ROUTLEDGE LIBRARY EDITIONS:
AGRIBUSINESS AND LAND USE

I0127739

Volume 20

THE COMMON AGRICULTURAL POLICY

THE COMMON AGRICULTURAL POLICY

Prospects for Change

JOAN PEARCE

Routledge
Taylor & Francis Group
LONDON AND NEW YORK

First published in 1981 by Routledge & Kegan Paul Ltd

This edition first published in 2024
by Routledge
4 Park Square, Milton Park, Abingdon, Oxon OX14 4RN

and by Routledge
605 Third Avenue, New York, NY 10158

Routledge is an imprint of the Taylor & Francis Group, an informa business

British Library Cataloguing in Publication Data
A catalogue record for this book is available from the British Library

ISBN: 978-1-032-48321-4 (Set)
ISBN: 978-1-032-48371-9 (Volume 20) (hbk)
ISBN: 978-1-032-48374-0 (Volume 20) (pbk)
ISBN: 978-1-003-38871-5 (Volume 20) (ebk)

DOI: 10.4324/9781003388715

Publisher's Note
The publisher has gone to great lengths to ensure the quality of this reprint but points out that some imperfections in the original copies may be apparent.

Disclaimer
The publisher has made every effort to trace copyright holders and would welcome correspondence from those they have been unable to trace.

Chatham House Papers · 13

The Common Agricultural Policy:
Prospects for change

Joan Pearce

The Royal Institute of International Affairs

Routledge & Kegan Paul
London, Boston and Henley

The Royal Institute of International Affairs is an unofficial body which promotes the scientific study of international questions and does not express opinions of its own. The opinions expressed in this paper are the responsibility of the author.

First published 1981
by Routledge & Kegan Paul Ltd
39 Store Street, London WC1E 7DD,
9 Park Street, Boston, Mass. 02108, USA and
Broadway House, Newtown Road,
Henley-on-Thames, Oxon RG9 1EN
Set by Hope Services, Abingdon and
printed in Great Britain by
Billing & Son Ltd., Guildford and Worcester

Pearce, Joan.
The common agricultural policy.
(Chatham House papers; no. 13)
Includes bibliographical references.
1. Agriculture and state – European Economic Community
countries.   I. Title.   II. Series.
HD1920.5.Z8P4 1981   338.1'84   81-17948

ISBN 0-7100-9069-2   AACR2

Contents

Acknowledgements

I should like to thank the many people in government departments, farm organizations, and others in the member states and the Commission who kindly discussed the CAP with me and provided the raw material on which much of this study was based. I am also most grateful for the comments I have received on this and earlier drafts, and in particular for help from Richard Portes. Special thanks are due to the staff of Chatham House, particularly to Lawrence Freedman for his patience, and to Jean Pell for unflaggingly typing many drafts.

J.P.

1 Introduction

Among the many surpluses generated by the CAP, there is a surplus of proposals for changing it. This paper is not intended to add to the number of these proposals, but will analyse some of them in the light of current developments in the European Economic Community. The central problem of the CAP is that it uses a single instrument, prices, to pursue two objectives: maintaining farm income; and balancing supply and demand. Neither objective has been adequately achieved. There is constant pressure to raise prices so as to ensure a decent income for low-income farmers, but high prices encourage output to expand, and so add to surpluses and thus to the budgetary costs of the CAP. Other costs are imposed on the Community by the CAP: it wastes economic resources; redistributes income inequitably; and causes large transfers of resources between member states.

The budgetary costs are receiving growing attention for various reasons: their uneven distribution among member states has resulted in proposals for changing the structure of the budget; the Community's financial resources seem likely to be exhausted some time before the end of 1983; and in 1984 there is likely to be a further rise in expenditure, since Spain and Portugal are due to become members of the Community then. Because the CAP accounts for such a large share of the budget, discussions about the budget inevitably involve the CAP. The forthcoming revisions to budgetary arrangements will entail changes in the CAP, but these changes could either improve or mar the prospects for reforming the CAP.

The paper begins by sketching the origins of the CAP, setting it in the broader context of the Community, and tracing its political and

1

institutional evolution. Chapter 3 describes the operation of the price system, shows how external relations and structural policy have been subordinated to it, and how it has dominated financing. In Chapter 4 the results of the CAP are compared with the five objectives set for it in the Treaty of Rome, and the extent to which member states have continued to pursue national objectives is demonstrated in Chapter 5. An assessment of the costs and benefits of the CAP, for the Community and for the rest of the world, is made in Chapter 6.

The last three chapters deal with the revision of the budget and its implications for the CAP. Chapter 7 outlines the pressures for budgetary reform, and considers some of the proposals that affect the CAP and the attitudes of the member states towards them. In Chapter 8, recent events, culminating in the publication of the Commission's report on restructuring the budget, will be described. Chapter 9 analyses the Commission's proposals and member states' initial reactions to them, indicates how events may develop in the next year or two, and suggests some objectives and tactics for the negotiations.

2 The political framework

The reasons for including agriculture in the European Economic Community were both political and economic: France would have declined to participate in a Community that provided for free trade in industrial goods but not in agricultural goods; and exclusion of agriculture would have distorted competition within industry because divergent food prices would have implied divergent wage rates. In addition, the agricultural sector was expected to demonstrate the advantages of collective action and so be a motor of integration. The founders of the Community believed that within the larger market a more efficient allocation of resources would be achieved. The consequent benefits to producers and consumers would generate political cohesion at the Community level comparable to that which the welfare state had generated at national level. Further, farmers were thought to be one of the various 'functional' groups whose common interests would transcend national boundaries and help to advance this process. To take the view that agriculture was a particularly suitable sector in which to promote integration was perhaps to make a virtue of necessity. Member states were unlikely to delegate to the Community responsibility for administering the prosperous and expanding sectors of their economies.[1]

The Treaty of Rome provided the Community with four main institutions: the European Commission; the Council of Ministers; the Parliament; and the Court of Justice. Of these, the first two were directly responsible for policy-making. The Commission is a collegiate body appointed for four years, whose fourteen members (since the admission of Greece in January 1981) are appointed by common consent of the member governments. They are required to act independently of member governments and of the Council of Ministers. Each Commissioner is responsible for a particular area of policy, but they are collectively responsible for all their decisions. The Commission has a dual role: first, as the guardian of the Treaty of Rome, it draws up proposals for Community policy; second, it acts as executive and secretariat, supported by a civil service organized in Directorates-General corresponding to the areas of responsibility of the Commissioners. The Directorate-General for Agriculture is commonly known as DG VI (the sixth Directorate-General).

On most issues the Council of Ministers has to negotiate to give the Commission's proposals the force of law. Each member government has a seat on the Council and may send any member of government it chooses to meetings. The Treaty of Rome provided for majority voting in the Council on many issues, after a twelve-year transition period. Presidency of the Council rotates among the member governments every six months. For some areas of policy special councils have evolved: the Agriculture Council, which comprises the agriculture ministers of the member states, normally meets once a month. The discussions of most councils are prepared by the Committee of Permanent Representatives (Coreper), which comprises member governments' ambassadors to the European Communities, but the Agriculture Council is served by the special Committee on Agriculture (SCA), which comprises agricultural officials.

In the same year that the Community was founded, 1958, the Comité des Organisations Professionelles Agricoles des Pays de la Communauté Economique Européenne (COPA) was set up, with the active encouragement of the Commission. This was a federation of farmers' unions in the Community. To qualify for membership of COPA, organizations had to meet two key criteria: they had to be national, i.e. not confined to one region, and general, i.e. not confined to one group of products. They were also expected to be representative of all farmers in their country and to be exclusively agricultural. COPA was to coordinate the positions of its member organizations. They provided notes from which COPA built up a common position. COPA could be seen as promoting that coalescence of functional interest at Community level which was to contribute to the process of integration.

Agriculture in the member states

Agriculture was economically and politically important in all six member states and already subject to widespread intervention. In the mid-1950s it accounted for more than a quarter of civilian employment and for more than 10 per cent of GNP. Size alone made agriculture politically important, and in most countries the political weight of landowners was greater than their numbers warranted.

For several reasons the member states, like many other developed countries, intervened extensively in their agricultural sectors, as well as affording them external protection. Agriculture's role as a provider of basic necessities had been thrown into relief by the food shortages that had occurred during and immediately after the Second World War. On both economic and strategic grounds, countries were anxious to safeguard food supplies. Yet more uncertainty surrounds production of food than of other goods because agriculture is peculiarly dependent on natural phenomena, such as climate and disease.

Despite its importance, agriculture in most European countries began to undergo a relative decline in the years following the Second World War as their economies became more prosperous. Increased per capita income may be matched by increased expenditure on food up to the point at which the capacity of the human stomach is reached and the desire for a higher quality or more varied diet is met. Subsequently, the income elasticity of demand for food is less than unity: that is, expenditure increases by a smaller proportion than income, or may even fall for certain products. To the extent that the agricultural sector does not reduce its costs or expand exports commensurately, it receives a smaller proportion of national income. Unless the number of individuals engaged in agriculture declines, their incomes fall relative to those in other sectors.

This occurs simultaneously with another aspect of economic expansion: technological advance. Whereas some farmers are well placed to benefit from this, others are not. The apparent solution is for those who are unlikely to gain from technological progress to move out of agriculture, leaving a smaller number to produce a larger amount. In fact a reduction in agricultural employment did occur, notably between 1950 and 1970, but there remain many older farmers with small farms, who are both less able to increase their income from agriculture and less able and willing to seek an alternative occupation. Furthermore, particularly in areas in which agriculture is the main activity, a reduction in agricultural employment often has adverse repercussions on the rural community as craftsmen and traders find that there is less demand for their goods and as social services become underutilized. The outcome may be rural depopulation, which is undesirable for political, social and environmental reasons, if not for economic ones.[2]

Member states' national agricultural policies reflected the importance accorded to the sector and to raising its productivity, as well as the desire to shield agricultural production from the detrimental effects of the natural conditions and the economic forces that impinged on it. Similar considerations determined *the five objectives* set for agricultural policy in the Treaty of Rome. These were: increased productivity; a fair standard of living for the farm population; stable markets; security of supplies; and reasonable prices for consumers. Although such objectives implied intervening to organize markets and to adapt production structures, the Treaty did not specify how the Community was to do this.

Although agriculture was important, faced similar problems and had similar objectives throughout the Community, there were wide disparities among the agricultural sectors and policies of member states. Within agriculture there was great diversity among member states relating to the type of land available for cultivation, the size of farms, yields, the importance of particular products, the extent of mechanization and the use of fertilizers, and the role of marketing and farmers' organizations. The relationship of agriculture to the economy as a whole also varied in terms of the proportion of land used, labour force employed and GNP generated by agriculture, as well as the degree of self-sufficiency. Furthermore, agricultural policy is affected by price and income levels, fiscal and financial institutions and the provision of social security, in all of which there were disparities among member states. Agricultural policy was applied by a motley collection of measures, including price guarantees, production quotas, denaturing of products or their transformation into alcohol, grubbing up of vines and fruit and outright import prohibitions.

Basic decisions on the CAP

Member states had already determined the priorities of agricultural policy and had developed, albeit chaotically, instruments with which to pursue them. Although governments were willing to hand over the administration of agricultural policy to a supranational authority, they wished to ensure that the economic and political interests which national policy aimed to protect would be at least as well protected by the Community. They approached the CAP with established but disparate circumstances, priorities and policies. With regard to the formulation of a framework for the CAP, the major dividing line was between countries that were net exporters of agricultural products and those that were net importers.

Of the exporters, the Netherlands was a small country with an efficient agriculture, which maintained an open trading system. France, however, a large country with a moderately efficient agriculture, used a combination of price support, production controls, export-stimulating measures and some non-tariff protection to maintain a delicate balance between production and demand. The largest importer, Germany, was a large country with an inefficient agriculture, which regulated the domestic price level by means of import controls. It was endeavouring to raise productivity, and production, and to ensure that the decline in its agricultural labour force did not have detrimental repercussions.[3]

The Treaty of Rome proposed that there should be a conference of officials and representatives of the agricultural sector in the six member states to define governing principles and policy for European agriculture. The conference, held at Stresa in 1958, expanded on the objectives set by the Treaty of Rome and indicated in general terms how they should be pursued. European agriculture was to be reformed and made competitive but without prejudicing the family character of the farm unit. Common agricultural prices, which were to be established progressively and to settle slightly above world market prices, were to remunerate farmers adequately without encouraging overproduction. The Community's agricultural policy could not be based on self-sufficiency, but there should be protection against unfair foreign competition.

Building on the conclusions of the Stresa conference, the Commission prepared proposals for the Common Agricultural Policy which underwent several amendments, notably the rejection by the Council of Ministers of strict organization of trade and markets based on quantitative restrictions. France pushed for, and eventually obtained, a highly standardized system. There would be a unified internal market with common prices, supported if necessary by intervention buying; variable levies on imports from third countries would ensure Community preference, that is, that Community exporters would have priority of access to the markets of Community importers; export restitutions would enable the Community's production to be exported to third countries; and member states would jointly finance the cost of intervention and export restitutions.

The policy which emerged and came into force in January 1962 embodied three major components: markets and prices; external relations; and structure. The markets and prices element proved to be by far the most important in the CAP, and the three principles on which this part of the policy was based are habitually referred to as *the three principles* of the CAP. They were: a unified market, implying common prices, which was to permit free circulation of goods; Community preference, which was to protect the unified market from imports and fluctuations in world markets by subjecting imports to levies that would ensure that their prices exceeded Community prices; and financial solidarity, whereby funding would be transferred from the national to the Community level through the European Agricultural Guidance and Guarantee Fund (FEOGA, from its French title).

Germany would have preferred a looser arrangement providing for coordination of national policies. For a limited but important range of products Germany maintained higher prices to help alleviate farm-income problems. The decision to apply common prices throughout the Community left Germany feeling it had little option but to insist that those prices be relatively high.

This original set of decisions about the CAP, taken in the early 1960s, had profound implications for the direction of the policy and for the negotiating process. They determined that the dominant feature of the CAP would be a price policy whose chief objective was to maintain farm income. Moreover, the combination of high and guaranteed prices for unlimited amounts of production, stringent protection against imports, and technical progress was bound to lead to overproduction. Common financing ensured that the financial consequences of overproduction were not met directly by the member states responsible for them. A decade and a half of empirical evidence has confirmed that as an economic policy for the Community as a whole the CAP was irrational.

But the continued existence of the CAP indicates that member states deemed that on balance it operated to their advantage. Net exporters believed that the opportunity offered by the CAP to increase production and exports unrestrictedly accelerated their economic growth and improved their balances of payments. Net importers derived few economic gains from the CAP but did obtain a means of maintaining farm income through price support, which was politically important in both Germany and Italy. For Germany, the economic drawbacks of the CAP could be set against the more favourable aspects of the Community, such as the expansion of industrial trade. Membership of the Community was a valuable asset in the conduct of Germany's foreign policy, particularly its relations with the Soviet Union and Eastern Europe. All the member governments had farming interests to satisfy, and the economic and financial costs of the policy that had been adopted were masked by the Community's increased bargaining power in trade and by continued economic growth. At least during the 1960s the idea of a European agricultural policy was politically popular with electorates.

Compromise among national interests not only determined the form of the CAP but also set the pattern for negotiations. Decisions were reached by means of package deals in which all member governments granted and obtained concessions. Often an atmosphere of crisis pervaded the process, the most extreme instance being in 1965, when France refused for six months to attend meetings of the Council of Ministers in protest against the Commission's proposals for the financing of the CAP. At a meeting in Luxembourg in January 1966 various points were settled, and it was agreed that all major policy decisions should require a unanimous vote by the Council (the Luxembourg compromise).

Proceedings were largely dominated by France and Germany. The smaller member states were sometimes able to exploit differences between these two and sometimes able to gain an advantage by being unobtrusive. Italy's dependence on Mediterranean products set it aside from the others and, rather than participating in the construction of a package, it tended to wait until one had been completed and then use blocking tactics to force the addition of items intended to benefit Mediterranean producers. The enlargement of the Community in 1973 complicated matters. Denmark and Ireland, as small countries that were net agricultural exporters, nestled comfortably into the CAP. The UK, on the other hand, like Germany, was a large net importer but, unlike Germany, had neither the political incentive nor the economic means to contribute sizably to the cost of the CAP. Although both countries' farm sectors were comparatively small, the UK had fewer and more efficient farmers than Germany. Futhermore, the UK had previously maintained farm income through direct payments to farmers rather than through price support, so that the CAP entailed unwelcome rises in consumer prices. The UK's problems were temporarily alleviated by monetary compensatory amounts (MCAs) and by transitional arrangements which ensured that it did not feel the full impact of the costs of the CAP until 1979.

The UK was not the only member state with reservations about the CAP, but the governments of those that had been involved from the outset were more conscious of the manner in which obligations and bargains had accumulated and more chary of making other than marginal changes. Rather than revising the CAP, they preferred to continue to pursue their national interests by seeking trade-offs within the CAP and by using national aids outside the CAP. Since the CAP had been chiefly confined to prices and markets, sizable scope was left to member states to apply their own non-price measures. In addition, from 1969 the system of MCAs allowed each member state to adjust the exchange rate used to calculate common prices in a way that gave it some control over domestic agricultural prices, while retaining the semblance of a common price system.

The role of the Commission

The Commission was uneasy about the member governments treating the CAP as an arena in which to strike bargains in the pursuit of national interest rather than to develop a communal approach. It was also aware that the price-support system being advanced by France was on its own an inadequate basis on which to build a Community policy. A dilemma confronted the Commission: either it could challenge the vested interests of the member states, at the risk of causing the CAP and possibly the Community to be stillborn; or it could accept that the CAP was to be shaped by a series of trade-offs among national interests, at the risk of delivering an economic policy that in Community terms was debilitating. The Commission chose to run the second of these risks, seemingly on the grounds that a start had to be made somewhere.[4] Once the competence of supranational institutions was more firmly established, the confidence of farmers was gained, and member states became aware of the consequences of the price-support system, it would be possible to adapt the CAP along more communal and more sensible lines. There was an element of self-seeking in this view, since the Commission saw the setting up of the CAP as a means of developing its own powers.

That the Commission succeeded in getting its proposals for price support and market organization accepted by all the member states was an achievement. But they did not heed its warnings about the consequences of heavy protection and higher prices, and its emphasis on the need to link the provisions for prices and markets with a rationalization of agriculture. In its efforts to place the CAP on a firmer footing, the Commission was frustrated in part by the Treaty of Rome. Member governments opposed to structural changes in agriculture exploited the Treaty's vagueness regarding the Commission's competence in structural policy. As guardian of the Treaty, the Commission was intended both to preserve it and to initiate policies for furthering its application, but the authority for this second function was less explicit.

In 1968, Sicco Mansholt, the vice-president of the Commission responsible for agriculture, pointed out that if the CAP continued to consist almost exclusively of a price-support system it would fail to accomplish its primary objective of maintaining farm income. Under his direction proposals were drawn up for reforming the structure of agricultural production. Although parts of the Mansholt Plan were eventually adopted, as an attempt to reform the CAP it was rejected. Subsequently the Commission's role as an initiator of innovative policies grew weaker. It developed an extensive network for consultation to ensure that any proposals it made would be broadly acceptable. Increasingly the Commission declined to contest the views of member governments; avowed that any change to the CAP should be gradual; and sought to justify rather than to criticize the CAP. At the same

11

time, links between Commissioners and their 'home' governments became closer, and the collegial principle wore thin.

As the Commission's political role diminished, its administrative role expanded. The implementation of the CAP required the setting up of extensive bureaucratic machinery. The variable import levies and export restitutions require detailed operation. The cereals levy, for example, has to be calculated each day, and the beef levy each week, and to be communicated by the Commission to the national organizations that act as agents for the Community. In technical matters, substantial legislative power has been delegated to the Commission acting on the advice of management committees. There is a management committee for each main group of products, appointed by member governments from among ministry officials or staff of national marketing organizations. The Commission submits to the management committees each year hundreds of draft decisions, the vast majority of which are adopted.[5] At the bureaucratic level the CAP is a Community policy by virtue of its scale of activity and the practical effects that it has throughout the Community. This enhances the prestige of DG VI by comparison with most other directorates-general, which have little scope for influencing either the formulation or the functioning of policy.

The price review

Since the chief element of the CAP is price policy, the main occasion for determining policy is the annual price review. Not only is there bargaining over prices but other measures are traded against price increases. The review, like other major policy proposals, is preceded by an extensive process of consultation. Commission officials are regularly in contact with member governments and their officials, and receive the views of various pressure groups. The draft proposal is submitted to the Commissioner responsible for agriculture, who in turn submits it for the collective approval of the Commission. It is then transmitted formally to the Council of Ministers and becomes in effect a public document, usually in December or January. An 'opinion' is given by the Economic and Social Committee, whose 143 members are drawn from trade unions, employers and professional organizations, and 'general interest' representatives, and by the European Parliament, whose Agri-

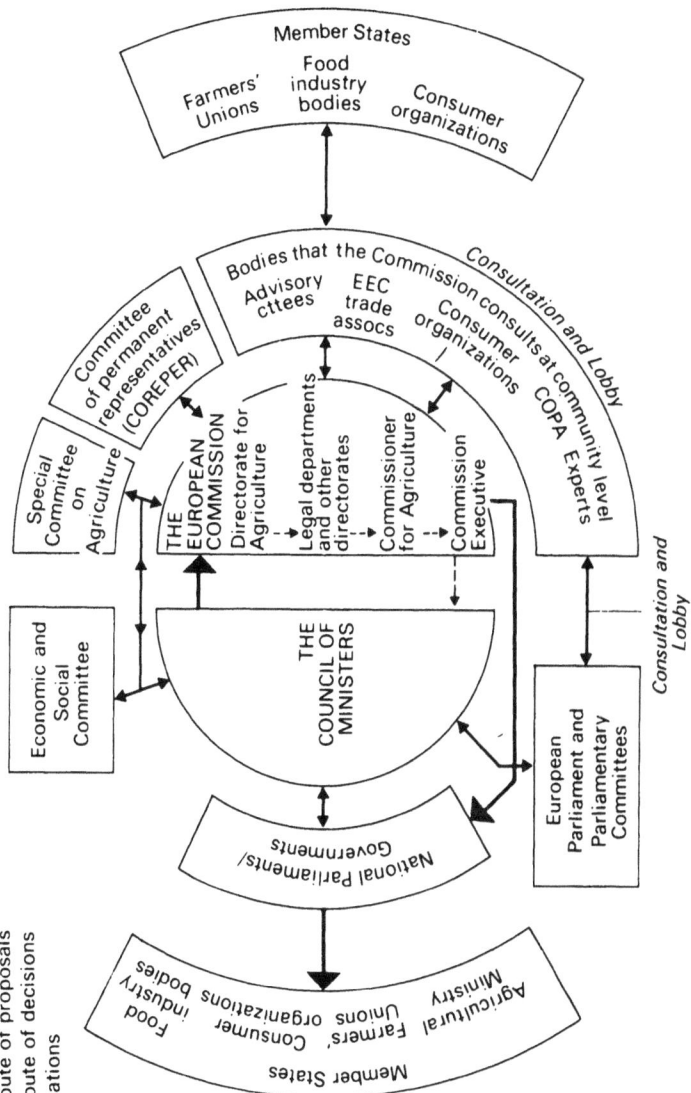

The decision-making process

Source: John S. Marsh and Pamela Swanney, *Agriculture and the European Community* (London: Allen & Unwin, for the University Association for Contemporary European Studies, 1980).

culture Committee presents its views, together with those of other committees, to a full session of the Parliament for approval (*see diagram*).

On the basis of the comments it receives, the Commission may at
any point revise the draft proposal. Before finally being presented to
the Agriculture Council in February, the proposal is examined by the
SCA. If the Council disagrees with the proposal, the Commission may
revise it to make it more acceptable. Deliberations have in some years
continued for as long as five months, though the aim is to reach a decision
before the beginning of the new marketing year, which for beef and
milk, two important products, is 1 April.[6]

The nature of the policy-making process, together with the emphasis
of the CAP on maintaining farm income through price support, has
effectively turned the annual price review into annual wage negotiations
for the farm sector. As a starting-point for its price proposals, the Commission uses the so-called 'objective method' to make a statistical
calculation of 'the average increase in CAP institutional prices needed
by "modern" Community farms if labour income on these farms is to
keep pace with average incomes in the non-agricultural sector'.[7] Developments in costs, income and exchange rates in each member state over a
three-year period are evaluated and then weighted to arrive at a figure
for the price increase required for the Community as a whole. The Commission describes the 'objective method' as a general indicator which it
uses with others to arrive at its final proposals. Other indicators include
the state of agricultural markets, the overall economic situation and
financial constraints. Probably the objective method has declined in
importance since it was introduced in the early 1970s.

The extensive consultation that accompanies the preparation of
proposals provides various opportunities for lobbying by interest
groups, both in Brussels and in national capitals, which the farm sector
in particular utilizes. COPA has become the orchestrator of comprehensive operations to further the well-being of farmers. Instead of co-
ordinating national positions, it now has a working group of experts
from member organizations which drafts policy proposals. These are
passed to the presidium, which comprises one representative from each
member organization and determines COPA's policy. COPA works
closely with the Commission in the preparation of the annual price
review. The working group of experts, the presidium and the Commis-

sioner responsible for agriculture meet for unofficial discussions, which are chiefly concerned with the objective method calculation.

During the formal consultation stage COPA intervenes at various levels. Besides making its own representations to the Commission, it approaches members of the Economic and Social Committee and of the European Parliament, in both of which farm interests are active. COPA's member organizations approach politicians and ministries in their respective countries. This dexterous exercise may be supplemented during the actual price negotiations by mass demonstrations by farmers themselves. Although consumers' organizations, food-processing industries and others press their cases through various channels, no other group exerts as much pressure at as many levels as do farmers.

Traditionally, agricultural policy was a specialized area which usually concerned only the sector itself and those ministers and officials directly responsible for it. Since the CAP was set up, agricultural policy has assumed broader significance because decisions are made jointly and because they result in transfers between countries. This has not lessened the close cooperation between the farm sector and the agriculture ministry in each member state. Agriculture ministers tend to feel that their first obligation is to their country's farm sector regardless of whether this is consistent with national interest. Furthermore, common financing gives them a greater freedom to take decisions entailing higher budgetary costs than they would have if the burden fell directly on their national exchequers. In the series of bargains that characterizes the negotiating process, agriculture ministers concentrate on exchanging advantages, in the form of price increases or other gains, for their farm sectors. Because of the practice that decisions must be unanimous, each minister can withhold concessions from the others. When the interests of member states' farm sectors conflict, there is often a struggle. There is sometimes collusion, however, since agriculture ministers appreciate the allegiance that each feels to the farm sector, and are willing to assist one another, particularly when national elections are imminent.

The approach to calculating price increases, the political organization of farmers, the inclinations of agriculture ministers, the financial arrangements and the nature of the negotiating process all conduce to large price increases. Under national policies price increases would be smaller, since no single country would have so many interests to accommodate, while thoroughly supranational policy would be less susceptible to individual interests. At the Community level, as at the national level, agricultural policy-making has been largely confined to a small group. The councils of foreign and finance ministers have failed to restrain the decisions of the Agriculture Council, while within national governments agriculture ministers have justified these decisions on the grounds that they were necessary to avoid a crisis in the Community.

The CAP and the Community

The CAP was not intended to be the Community's only common policy, but failure to develop other policies has meant that it is the only internal policy in which the Commission has powers of active management and the member governments are bound to act in common. For its role as a motor of integration the CAP has constructed a large body of machinery. The means by which a complex common price system and tightly protectionist instruments are administered are for the most part imposing. As well as the Community's institutions, the organization built up by the farm sector is impressive.

The CAP has not, however, been the force for integration that was intended. In part the CAP originated in the need to provide outlets in the Community for French agricultural exports so as to gain France's agreement to the setting up of the Community. For similar reasons the structure of the CAP was largely of French design. Common prices were to prevent high-cost producers in the Community from asking higher prices; Community preference was to give agricultural exporters prior access to Community markets; and common financing was to ensure that if production exceeded Community requirements, the cost of disposal would be shared. In the long run, because Germany insisted on a relatively high level of common prices, the purpose of the design was foiled.

Initially, net exporters gained by high prices and Community preference, since they were able to increase both the value and the volume of their exports. Prices were set high enough, however, that high-cost producers were not eliminated. In fact high prices, together with price support and Community preference, encouraged greater self-sufficiency in net importing countries. Italy is the only member state that has become less self-sufficient since joining the Community (*see Table 12*). Because of Community preference, greater self-sufficiency of Community importers first squeezes third-country exporters out of their markets; subsequently Community exporters are affected. If export opportunities within the Community cease expanding, then either production too has to cease expanding or the cost of disposing of excess production rises.

The CAP is regarded in France as an achievement that should be stoutly defended. Reference is often made to the growth in France's agricultural production and exports, and to the consequent benefits to national income and the balance of payments that have occurred in the past two decades. France's share in the Community's agricultural production has been stable, however, and agricultural exports to the Community as a percentage of France's total agricultural exports are stagnating while imports are rising (*see Table 13*). Since the CAP began to work less to France's benefit within the Community, France has been pressing for the Community to adopt a more aggressive export policy towards third countries. Had prices been lower, France should have been able to obtain a larger share of the Community's market. Also, Community prices would have been closer to world prices so that export restitutions would have been less costly.

A further reason for including agriculture in the Community was to avoid distortions within industry that could result from member states having different national agricultural policies. The CAP, in relying heavily on one policy instrument, has left national governments wide discretion in other areas of agricultural policy. In addition, thanks to MCAs, common prices operated only from 1967 to 1969.

The CAP was also supposed to facilitate specialization and so raise income to the benefit of consumers and producers. It has failed to do so because the decision to maintain farm income by supporting prices, together with the high level of prices, has meant that price competition has been inadequate to bring about a significant reallocation of resources within agriculture. Moreover, the CAP has resulted in resources being retained in agriculture, where they have been less productive than they could have been in another sector. Evidence of this is the fact that the Community produces more than can be sold at the price it has set. The CAP allotted to prices two functions: balancing supply and demand and so helping to allocate resources efficiently; and redistributing income. They could not perform both functions and have performed neither satisfactorily. Price support has resulted in excess production. It has effected a transfer of income to farmers from consumers, but the wealthier farmers have gained the most, while the poorer consumers have suffered the most.

Farmers were the functional group whose concurrence of interests was to prompt them to advance the process of specialization, which would raise the income of agriculture and of the Community as a whole, so bringing benefits that would promote the Community ethos. The decision to maintain income by price support has meant that farmers have demonstrated their common purpose by pressing for price increases. They have also united to oppose reform of the CAP. There are, however, issues that divide the farm sector, because of conflicts of interest between producers in different countries or of different products, and these the CAP has not mitigated.

While the CAP has not generated integration in the way that was envisaged, a folklore has grown up which depicts the CAP as it was intended to be. The CAP has succeeded in fulfilling its objectives and has acted as a unifying force. Since the CAP has become a cornerstone of the Community, to change it without creating other common policies would be seen as undermining the Community. Agriculture's special status has been reinforced: it is politically and economically important not only at national level but also at Community level. Most folklores absorb new facts in a manner consistent with their basic theme. In the case of the CAP this has extended to economic concepts. Terms such as surplus and market balance have been used, not in the accepted sense but in a sense that helps to justify the internal logic of the CAP.

Whereas the framework and rationale of the CAP are supranational, in substance it amounts to a coordination of national policies. For nation-states to coordinate their policies in a mutually beneficial way is a worthwhile undertaking. That it is not the common purpose for which the CAP was established, and which it still purports to pursue, might not seem to matter. The common framework, however, impedes a constructive coordination of national polices.

The motor of integration has run out of control. The CAP does not serve common objectives, nor does it permit national policies to be concerted. It imposes increasing costs on the Community budget and on the national economies. Yet to change it so as to reassert control is difficult. Member states that are net exporters of agricultural products consider that they derive economic benefits from the CAP. Most member governments and political parties remain convinced that the farm sector is politically important, and most farmers are opposed to any radical change in the CAP. Those governments that would like to see the system changed are cautious about making more than peripheral alterations to the intricate network of trade-offs, both within the CAP and between it and other policy areas, that has been built up. One set of pressures for change that member states will have to tackle are those emanating from the budget. The later chapters of this paper consider whether they are likely to be dealt with in a way that would restore control over the CAP. First there is a chapter which describes the machinery of the CAP, and then three chapters which attempt to assess it by considering its results in terms of Community objectives, the ways in which member states have continued to pursue national objectives, and the CAP's cost and benefits.

3 The machinery of the CAP

Markets and prices

From the outset, markets and prices dominated the CAP. Once the three principles had been laid down, the Commission began to define, and to submit to the Council of Ministers for approval, the market organization for each product. Agreement was reached on six products in time to implement a policy on 1 January 1962, and on a further four products in December 1963. The Commission then turned its attention to establishing common prices throughout the Community.

The market organizations now fall into four categories, distinguished by the type of mechanisms they use: internal price support and external protection cover over 70 per cent of production (cereals, sugar, most dairy products, beef and veal, pigmeat, some fruit and vegetables, table wines, fish products); external protection alone covers 25 per cent (eggs, poultrymeat, most cheese, flowers, rice, other fruit and vegetables, other wines); additional product aid, such as deficiency payments and production subsidies, covers 2.5 per cent (durum wheat, olive oil, certian oilseeds, tobacco); and flat-rate aid covers 0.6 per cent (cottonseed, flax and hemp, hops, silkworms, seed and dehydrated fodder).

Both internal price support and external protection are directed towards maintaining a desired price level for Community producers. A price is set annually for the wholesale market in each product 'to enable farmers to plan production and give economic guidance to all market users'. At a certain percentage (differing among products) below this price there is a floor price (or intervention price), at which intervention agencies are obliged to buy any production that cannot be sold at a higher price.[1] Intervention agencies were intended to safeguard market stability by buying up products that were temporarily in surplus and selling them at a later date, but because they were bound to buy all the production offered them, they became a means of ensuring that however much a farmer produced he was certain of being able to sell it, albeit at the relatively low intervention price.

There are some important differences in the degree to which different products are supported. The amount of price support a product receives is determined by the level of the desired price, the margin between it and the intervention price, and precisely how intervention operates. The desired price goes by various names, reflecting differences in the organization of products. For cereals, sugar, dairy products, olive oil, colza and sunflower seed, it is a target price; for beef, veal and wine, a guide price; for pigmeat and fruit and vegetables, a basic price; and for tobacco, a norm price. The explanation for the distinctions is partly that particular markets function differently and partly that some products were thought to need more support because demand for them was not responsive to changes in price, so that when their price falls, producers are not compensated by a rise in demand. In practice, support has gone to northern products rather than southern products, to cereals rather than livestock and consequently (except in the case of milk) to large farms rather than small ones.

External protection is accorded from imports as well as to exports. A levy is imposed on imports to ensure that they are not sold below the desired price. Given that world prices fluctuate, the levy has to vary if prices inside the Community are to be stable: the lower world prices are, the larger is the variable levy. For cereals, sugar, dairy products and olive oil a threshold price is set, which is a little lower than the target price to allow for the cost of unloading and transport. The variable levy makes up the difference between the import price and the threshold price (*see diagram*). The calculation uses the lowest import price offered to the Community, but the same levy is charged on all consignments, whatever their price. The arrangements for other products embody the same general principle, though they are technically different and involve different amounts of support.

To enable Community exporters to sell on the world market, a refund or restitution can be paid to bridge the gap between Community

21

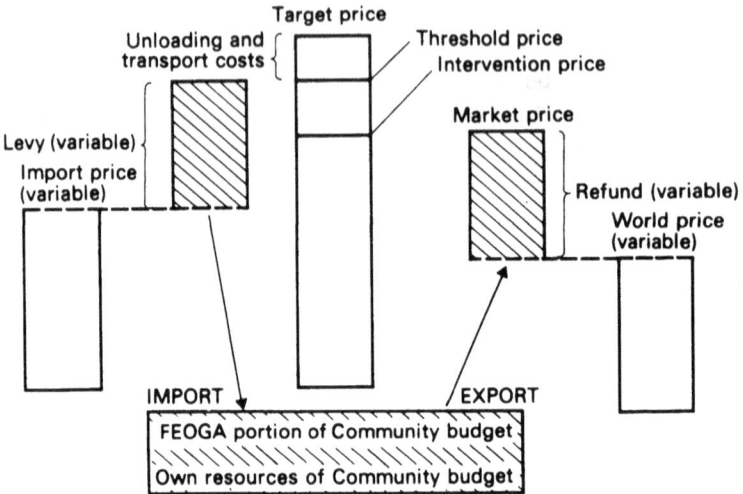

Levy and refund system for wheat

Adapted from Commission of the European Communities, *The Agricultural Policy of the European Community*, 2nd edition (Luxembourg: Office for Official Publications of the European Communities, 1979).

prices and lower world prices. The amount of the refund is determined by the management committee responsible for that particular product in the light of world prices, the size of the domestic surplus, and expected future trends. Should world prices rise above Community prices, an export tax (the counterpart of the variable import levy) may be imposed, which deters exports and restrains Community prices from following world prices up.

Having established the framework of the market organizations for the major products, the Community set about deciding what level of common prices should replace the disparate price levels prevailing in the member states. In the absence of a common currency, prices were set in a unit of account which, until 1971, was equivalent to one US dollar. The first product to be considered was cereals, which account for a large proportion of total farm production, since they make up a substantial part both of food for human consumption and of fodder for livestock, particularly pigs and poultry. In laying the foundations of the market organizations, the Community had decided to maintain farm income by supporting market prices, and in establishing common prices it was guided by this decision. The countries with high cereal prices (Germany, Italy and Luxembourg) were unwilling to reduce them by the full amount that would have been needed to bring them down to the level of the countries with low cereal prices (France, Belgium and the Netherlands). A compromise solution was reached in December 1964, which entailed increases for low-price countries and sizable reductions for high-price countries.

The common target prices for cereals that were applied from July 1967 were higher than the weighted average of cereal prices in the member states and much higher than world prices. Furthermore, the level of cereal prices ciritically influenced the level of prices for other products in two ways. First, if the relationship between the prices of different products were changed, some types of production would become relatively more profitable and farmers would tend to move into those and out of others. Second, since cereals are the chief item of current expenditure incurred by most livestock farmers, cereal prices are a major determinant of these farmers' costs and consequently of the price they need to obtain for their product in order to maintain their income. Hence, having set common prices for cereals at a relatively high level, the Community proceeded to set the common prices for other products, which came into effect in 1968, at related levels.

As well as maintaining farm income, common prices were intended to ensure that supply and demand within the Community were balanced. When the CAP was set up, the Community was self-sufficient in butter and some vegetables but was a net importer of other products. The member states had recently experienced, in the Second World War and its aftermath, food shortages and rationing. Consequently much importance was attached to ensuring security of supply. Since for most agricultural products variations in price have relatively little influence on demand, and since the Community's population was growing only slowly, demand changed relatively little. Ensuring market balance meant setting a price which would ensure that supply was adequate to meet a roughly fixed level of demand.

The Treaty of Rome did not specify what proportion of supply was to come from imports. By the late 1960s it was clear that in some products there was excess production. The method proposed for dealing with this was to limit output to self-sufficiency plus production that could be exported without a subsidy, and to change relative prices in favour of those products in which the Community was less than self-sufficient. Security of supply was then equated with complete self-sufficiency. This justified defining 'market balance' as a situation where Community supply equalled Community demand, 'surpluses' as net exports that required subsidies and 'deficits' as net imports.

High and guaranteed prices, together with improved productivity, continued to encourage production to increase. In some products, notably dairy products, sugar and cereals, the Community exceeded self-sufficiency. As surpluses developed, ensuring market balance ceased to be an argument for raising prices, but the political and social arguments for maintaining farm income predominated. Because real prices remained high, surpluses grew further and became an increasing burden on the Community budget, from which the cost of disposing of them has to be covered through paying for storage, for destruction or for export restitutions.

External relations

In the context of the CAP the role of external relations has been secondary to that of prices and markets. This reflects not only the CAP's order of priorities but also that of most countries' agricultural policies, which are similarly geared to internal objectives. Because domestic policy dictates that markets be managed and protected from external effects, most countries' participation in the world market is a residual, particularly for the United States and the EEC. Whereas industrial trade is based on an exchange of goods among nations, trade in temperate agricultural products is used to dispose of production that is surplus to domestic requirements, or to make up shortfalls in domestic production. The residual character of agricultural trade means that goods may be sold at scarcely more, or even less, than their cost of production, so that world prices are often much lower than they would be if exports took place only on commercial terms. It also means that world trade is a comparatively small proportion of world production (*see Table 14*). Since the world market is small in relation to domestic markets, minor shifts in production and consumption in domestic markets can significantly affect the world market. In the case of the

EEC this impact on the world market is amplified by the nature of the variable import levy (*see below, pp. 59–60*).

The Community has taken the line that, in view of the low prices and instability which characterize world agricultural markets, it needs to be cushioned, though not isolated, from them. Agricultural goods have been included in many of the Community's international trade commitments: bilateral agreements with the EFTA states and some countries in Latin America and the Mediterranean; the GATT multilateral trade negotiations; the generalized system of preferences granted to developing countries; and the Lomé Convention agreed with a group of countries in Africa, the Caribbean and the Pacific (ACP) that were former dependencies of member states.

In very few of these undertakings, however, have significant concessions been made on the temperate-zone agricultural products that are produced by the Community. The major exception occurred following the first enlargement of the Community, when certain traditional suppliers to the British market were allowed some measure of continued access for sugar, beef and butter.[2] Although the Community concluded agreements with a number of Mediterranean countries, an accord with Spain was not reached, and efforts to negotiate an overall policy for the Mediterranean have proved arduous. As with the current negotiations about Spain joining the Community, the main stumbling-block has been agricultural products, notably fruit and vegetables, and wine.

When the CAP was first set up, the Community consented to some modifications to make it compatible with the GATT (General Agreement on Tariffs and Trade). Subsequently the Community held that the CAP was an internal policy outside the scope of the GATT. In the Tokyo Round of negotiations it was agreed not to challenge the CAP on condition that the Community did not use subsidies to expand beyond its existing export markets.

By imposing a generally protectionist stance on external relations, the CAP's markets and prices element has, with the help of technical progress, caused the Community to become more self-sufficient and to increase its exports. As a result, exporters in non-EEC countries have found that as an export market for temperate-zone products the Community has continued to be relatively closed and has also been shrinking, and at the same time competition in other export markets has stiffened because of the Community's growing participation. Nor have developing countries that import food benefited from the Community's surpluses to the extent that might have been hoped, since food aid has been oriented more to the Community's need to dispose of surpluses than to the needs of recipients.

Structure

The structure of agriculture, that is the size of farms, level of employment, amount of capital and so forth, has never assumed the importance that it was intended to have in the CAP. At the outset, expenditure on the Guidance Section of FEOGA was to amount to up to one-third of that on the Guarantee Section. Finance was available for individual projects that furthered the objectives of the CAP or for solutions to specific problems of production or marketing. This was less a common policy than an ill-defined coordination of national policies. Furthermore, the rapid rise in guarantee expenditure which occurred in the mid-1960s resulted in a ceiling being imposed on guidance expenditure from 1967.

The drawbacks to using price policy to maintain farm income were already evident. Agriculture was a sector in relative decline, as indicated above (*p. 5*): rising per capita income led to a fall in the share of food in household budgets and hence to agriculture receiving a smaller proportion of national income. It should be noted that a farm's income is the difference between the revenue received for its output and the costs of its inputs, and can be increased in one of three ways: by raising output or prices and so increasing revenue; by reducing the number of farms so that individual farms are larger, account for a larger share of output and receive a larger share of revenue; or by lowering the costs per unit of output.

The difficulty with using price increases to maintain income is that within the farm sector producers do not incur uniform costs.[3] On the whole, high-cost producers are those with small farms, since small-scale production generally entails high unit costs and is less able to take advantage of technical progress to raise output. The price level that is needed to maintain even a modest income for a high-cost producer encourages a low-cost producer to expand output, which raises the cost of price support, while the high-cost producer still cannot expand. As long as price policy continues to maintain income, albeit scantily for the poorest farmers, there is inadequate incentive for farmers to respond to structural policy by leaving the sector or modernizing their farms to reduce costs. The experience of the 1960s demonstrated the reluctance of small farmers to leave the sector. During the decade employment in agriculture fell by one-third. Most of those who left were hired workers. Doubtless in the prosperous economic conditions of the 1960s they found more highly paid jobs outside agriculture. By 1970 only 26 per cent of those employed in agriculture were hired workers. The number of farmers declined by much less, so there was comparatively little change in the number and size of farms: the total number of farms was reduced by 11.3 per cent, and the number that were smaller than 5 hectares by 14.4 per cent between 1960 and 1967.

That price policy was a dog in the manger with regard to structural problems – not only failing to alleviate them but preventing their solution by other means – was recognized in the *Memorandum on the Reform of Agriculture in the European Economic Community*, more commonly known as the Mansholt Plan. The Plan attempted to point out that, without an increase in the size of farms and a reduction in their number, farm income would be a perennial problem. It contained comprehensive proposals for reforming the structure of production: financial incentives that would encourage farmers to take up various options, including continued ownership of land for those who ceased farming, early retirement and training for alternative employment; regional development schemes that would create new jobs in agricultural areas and so avoid rural depopulation; financial assistance for the development of larger, more economic farms that would be created by expansion of existing farms, a process of amalgamation and voluntary cooperation among farmers; withdrawal of some land from cultivation, mostly for reafforestation, which would reduce the Community's net imports of timber; adjustments to the organization of marketing to give farmers greater responsibility; and price reductions, principally in the dairy sector, which was the one with the most acute surplus problem.[4]

The initial budgetary cost of the Mansholt Plan would have been high, but would have declined in the second half of the 1970s, whereas the budgetary cost of price support was likely to increase indefinitely. Moreover, the Mansholt Plan would entail lower economic costs to the economy than did price support. The publication of the Plan, late in 1968, initiated an active and lengthy debate, from which it emerged that the farmers' organizations were firmly opposed to its radical proposals while member states' governments were concerned about its budgetary cost, though the Netherlands government in particular was sympathetic.

It was superseded by the 'mini-Mansholt' Plan which, after further trimming, resulted in 1972 in three directives. These dealt with modernization of farms, encouragement for small farmers to cease production and reorganization of their farms in larger units, and assistance for training in agricultural skills. The measures have not been very successful. Since they were directives (as opposed to regulations), each member state could choose how to apply them, and the result was that they were slowly, patchily and poorly implemented (*see Table 7*). Although a respectable number of modernization plans was submitted, they came mostly from larger farms, not the small farms that were meant to be the chief beneficiaries; up to the end of 1977 there were none from Italy, while 30 per cent of the funds had been disbursed in Germany. The response to inducements to cease farming was disappointing, and only in France, Germany and Ireland did the systems of land ownership and tenure facilitate reorganization of farms. At the end of 1977 four member states had yet to give effect to the third directive, and France accounted for more than half the people who had received training under it.

Experience suggests that there are major obstacles to structural change which structural policy may not be able to overcome. Farmers are unable or unwilling to leave the land in some regions because there is no alternative employment; farmers may lack the skills required for other work; and throughout the Community, recession has reduced job opportunities. The possibilities for increasing the productivity of small farms are limited because economies of scale cannot be applied. The range of products that can be produced on a small farm is limited. Many small farmers keep to dairy products because these, unlike other products, bring in a regular monthly income. As long as there is a large number of small farmers whose income is maintained solely by price support, the CAP will be increasingly costly. High and protected prices will encourage larger producers to raise output, but increased output will not lead to lower prices, because high prices will still be needed to maintain the income of small producers.

In recent years structural measures have been used less as an economic policy to encourage increased productivity than as a social and regional policy to assist poorer farmers and poorer regions of the Community. Finn Olav Gundelach, the Commissioner responsible for agriculture until January 1981, described the purpose of structural policy as being to 'make it more tolerable from the social and regional point of view to conduct the type of price policy which the market situation demands'.[5] A directive adopted in 1975 identified mountain and hill farmers, and those in other specified less-favoured areas, as suffering permanent natural handicaps, and aimed to compensate them. In 1978 a package of measures to assist the Mediterranean regions of the Community was introduced, which included aid for marketing and infrastructure projects. This package was a response to pressure from Italy. It reflected recognition that the price policy was biased in favour of northern products, that the Community would soon include three more Mediterranean countries, and that the Mediterranean regions faced particular problems: a large proportion of the population engaged in agriculture; a high level of underemployment; low labour productivity; and low income.

Finance

Common financing is one of the three principles of the CAP. Its significance derives partly from the political commitment that it implies. Furthermore, France contended that commonly financed price support was necessary to ensure free trade, because without it member states whose prices tended to be higher would be tempted to erect trade barriers against imports from those whose prices were lower. In 1971 it was agreed that the Community budget, including FEOGA, should have its own resources instead of being financed by contributions from national exchequers. These own resources comprise agricultural import levies, customs duties and a proportion of member states' VAT receipts (*see below, p. 67*).

The FEOGA has always been by far the largest item of Community expenditure, amounting to some 70 per cent of the total. Within the

FEOGA, the Guarantee Section takes up the vast majority of expenditure (more than 95 per cent). Originally the ratio between the Guarantee Section, which supports prices through intervention and export refunds, and the Guidance Section, which supports structural measures, was intended to be 3 to 1. In 1967 a ceiling was placed on the Guidance Section and, though this has been successively raised, the section has since 1975 always accounted for less than 5 per cent of the FEOGA.[6] A large part of guarantee expenditure inevitably goes to products that are in surplus (*see Table 6*). In 1979, almost 70 per cent was spent on three products (dairy, 43.4 per cent; cereals, 15 per cent; sugar, 9 per cent), which accounted for only 33.7 per cent of total production (respectively, 19.5 per cent, 11.5 per cent, 2.7 per cent).

Whereas the Guarantee Section finances all price support, the Guidance Section finances only 25 per cent of most structural measures, the balance being paid by member states. The 1980 Report on *The Agricultural Situation in the Community* (p. 85) states that it is impossible to ascertain precisely the expenditure by member states on Community measures. It is, however, clear that national expenditure on agricultural policy totals rather more than FEOGA expenditure, or twice as much if the financing of farmers' social security is included (*see Table 8*). There are sizable differences in the amounts spent by member states, which are not related to differences in the importance of agriculture in their economies. Member states also differ in their allocation of funds to different types of agricultural expenditure (*see below, p. 48*). The variegated pattern of agricultural expenditure in the Community reflects the predominance of price policy within the CAP and the fact that other aspects of agricultural policy are still largely determined by individual member states, in accordance with national resources and national objectives.

4 The objectives of the CAP

The CAP is less a monolith than an expanse of crazy paving. It is an assemblage of market organizations, whose common feature is price support, and of a few limited structural measures. Individuals and groups directly affected by the CAP often focus only on specific parts of it. Their view of the whole may be selective and inconsistent. Those who observe the CAP from a more distant standpoint may achieve greater coherence but risk losing sight of the political dimension.

One criterion for assessing the CAP is the extent to which it has achieved the five objectives set by the Treaty of Rome. Although the objectives are not disputed, differing intentions are ascribed to them. Furthermore, judgements may vary according to which data are used and how they are interpreted. Whatever the degree of success or failure in fulfilling the objectives, there remains the question of how much is attributable to the CAP.

Increased agricultural productivity

Labour productivity has increased as a result of capital investment, technical progress and a decline in the labour force, though these were only partly due to the CAP (*see Table 2*). Despite this improvement within agriculture, there was scarcely any change in its performance in relation to the rest of the economy. In no country has the ratio between output per worker in agriculture and in the whole economy risen significantly (*see Table 1*).

Besides promoting technical progress, the CAP was to ensure 'the rational development of agricultural production and the optimum

31

utilization of the factors of production'. Neither of these last two has been accomplished. This failure has been due to the excessive reliance on price support and also to the uneven distribution of support among products. The Commission acknowledged in 1975 that 'To seek to attain the objective of improved productivity solely by the operation of market and pricing policies is not only vain but, in the last analysis, involves a contradiction, for, in order to support incomes, it is necessary to fix prices at a high enough level to provide a living for the marginal farms.'[1]

A fair standard of living

The text of the Treaty of Rome indicated that there was a link between the first and second objectives of the CAP: increased productivity was the means by which 'to ensure a fair standard of living for the agricultural community, in particular by increasing individual earnings'. This link was already loosened at the Stresa conference, and subsequently the decision was taken to use price support to maintain farm income. As a result small-scale farmers were less inclined to leave the sector, though those with larger farms were encouraged to invest in more capital, with the effects on productivity that were described in the preceding section. The Mansholt Plan attempted to shift the emphasis back to productivity but failed.

The calculation of farm income is complicated. Farm income is the return to a business undertaking. Account has to be taken of revenues, benefits in kind, and the costs of inputs, including an imputed wage and return on capital for the farmer. Because farm income is not simply a wage or salary, difficulties also arise in comparing it with most non-farm incomes. Such comparisons partly depend on the performance of the rest of the economy: farmers in a country whose economy has expanded, such as Germany, may have fared relatively less well than those in a country with a sluggish economy, such as Britain.[2] Agricultural incomes have risen at a rate that is only slightly higher than in the economy as a whole, and so remain substantially below incomes in other sectors. In addition, there is no evidence that the dispersion of farm incomes, either within countries or between countries, has been reduced.

32

Market stability

Although one of the reasons frequently adduced for having an agricultural policy is that agriculture is peculiarly subject to natural conditions and economic forces which cause sizable and unpredictable variations in the volume of supply, the pursuit of market stability has concentrated entirely on price and not on quantity. Market stability, in this sense, has been unequivocally achieved for those products that receive price support, which number about three-quarters of the total. The high level of protection has narrowed price fluctuations in the Community's markets while amplifying those in world markets. Internal producer prices have been supported by the intervention system, which ensures that, whatever the quantity supplied, prices do not fall below a floor price, and, if stocks are adequate, is able to moderate price rises when supply falls short. The Community market is insulated from the world market by the variable import levy, which maintains a constant price for imports into the Community regardless of demand and supply conditions, and hence prices, in the rest of the world. This holds unless world prices are higher than Community prices, when the import levy may be replaced by an export tax. The variable import levy has also insulated domestic consumers from the consequences of domestic supply variations, in that when there has been a shortage in domestic supply that could be made up by imports, the price inside the Community has not risen.

In fact, in pursuing market stability through price stabilization, the Community went so far in separating prices from market conditions that the relation between quantities supplied and demanded was destabilized. The intervention system, though intended to even out fluctuations in supply by buying up production in times of surfeit and selling it in times of scarcity, in practice provided an unlimited price guarantee. Together with the variable import levy, it insulated producers from the effects of changes in supply and demand in Community and world markets. Given the high price level, this stimulated the emergence of surpluses. To dispose of these the Community has resorted to export refunds and to denaturing products.[3] In times of acute difficulty it has also prohibited imports and destroyed output or factors of production (by slaughtering dairy cows or grubbing up fruit trees). These measures have involved costs to the Community, in terms of budget expenditure and wasted economic resources, and to the rest of the world, in terms of reduced export outlets, lower prices and greater instability.

Security of supply

Security of supply has also undeniably been attained. Guaranteed high prices have encouraged increased production. The Treaty of Rome did not specify what level of self-sufficiency in which products constituted security of supply. Conventionally it is taken to mean 100 per cent self-sufficiency in all major products of the Community.

A concept of supply security that included some imports would imply lower price levels than are necessary to achieve self-sufficiency. To a small extent Community supply has encompassed imports, in that traditional suppliers have been given access to the Community for limited amounts of some products (*see above, p. 25*). Domestic producers, however, have pressed for these to be reduced or eliminated. The argument used against relying on imports, for example from New Zealand, is that in time of war supplies could be cut off. In assessing supply dependency, however, the appropriate criterion is the amount needed to survive, not the amount needed to maintain stable patterns of consumption. Furthermore, increased agricultural production in the Community has been associated with greater dependence on other imports, for example energy, which could equally be cut off in time of war.[4]

Even by the standard of 100 per cent self-sufficiency, the CAP has more than ensured the security of supplies. The Community has reached this level in virtually all those agricultural commodities that could be produced in Europe without price support, and has substantially exceeded it in a number of products (*see Table 12*).

Consumer prices

The fifth objective was to ensure that supplies reached consumers at reasonable prices. Consumer prices are only partly determined by producer prices. In the United Kingdom, agricultural raw materials account for about half the retail value of food; the other half arises in processing and distribution, and comprises labour, fuel, packaging and so forth.[5] Furthermore, these costs vary among member states, so that uniform producer prices do not necessarily mean that consumer prices are uniform across the Community.

The existence of surpluses indicates that consumers in the Community are paying higher prices than they need to obtain the supply of goods that they desire. High prices are defended on the grounds that they secure price stability. From the consumers' point of view, however, it might have been preferable to have a somewhat lower average price with somewhat less stability. It is also argued that since expenditure on food has declined as a percentage of total consumer spending, consumers are well able to pay higher prices, and that in return they have benefited from more varied and higher-quality food and from the amenities afforded by the maintenance of a traditional style of agriculture. The former benefit might have been obtained more cheaply from the world market; the latter is difficult to quantify. The 'ability-to-pay' argument ignores that those with low incomes are the least able to pay and spend proportionately more on food than the rest of the population.

To say that all five objectives of the Treaty of Rome have been achieved it is necessary at least to rephrase the last one. The Commission in a recent document said that 'security of food supplies, satisfaction of consumers' requirements, increased productivity and higher farm incomes have been achieved'.[6] Even this restatement is justified only on the grounds of quantity and quality, not of price. Equally it can be said that productivity and farm income have risen absolutely but not relative to the rest of the economy, that market stability and security of supply have been taken to ridiculous and damaging extremes, and that consequently consumers have paid prices which were not reasonable.

These differing assessments reflect differing views of what should have been the balance of priorities and the means of achieving the objectives. The decision to make farm income the chief priority and to maintain it by price support largely determined how far the CAP was able to fulfil all five objectives. From it followed the high and protected price level that ensured an exaggerated version of market stability and security of supply at the expense of consumers' interests. Because high prices tended to keep even the less efficient farmers on the land, increases in productivity and in individual earnings have been modest.

While the maintenance of farm income has been the CAP's primary objective, the effect of the CAP on farm income is difficult to ascertain. The CAP operates on farm income through price policy and structural policy. Several factors, other than price rises decided within the CAP and non-price measures in the CAP, can affect the net value added of agriculture: support measures undertaken by member states independently of the CAP; physical productivity such as milk and crop yields; and input prices.[7] Some of these have been directly influenced by the CAP, such as the prices of inputs produced by the agricultural sector. On the other hand, prices of inputs of non-agricultural origin, such as machinery and fuel, have evidently been determined primarily by supply-side influences (costs) beyond the scope of the CAP.

It is unrealistic to posit as an alternative to the CAP a free-market system that left prices and trade in agricultural goods to be determined solely by market forces. Whether at national or at Community level, policies would have been designed to administer agricultural markets in the pursuit of objectives comparable to those of the CAP. How national policies might have evolved is suggested by the policies of member states before they joined the Community. In the absence of the CAP, Germany might have kept agricultural prices at a higher level and France at a lower level; Britain might have continued some system of producer subsidies which used taxation rather than price support to maintain farm incomes. To infer what would have resulted from an alternative common policy is more problematic. This will be considered later in discussing the various proposals for adjusting or reorganizing the CAP.

5 National interests and the CAP

The five objectives may constitute the manifesto of the CAP, but its basic tenets are the three principles: a unified market with common prices; Community preference; and financial solidarity. A document concerning the CAP that fails to endorse these principles is liable to be rejected out of hand in agricultural circles. Officials in agriculture ministries and farmers' organizations throughout the Community almost invariably preface any remarks about the CAP by affirming the need to uphold its three principles. Yet it is questionable whether the spirit, if not the letter, of the principles has been observed. Member states have pursued national interests not only within the framework of the CAP – for example, by seeking to gain maximum advantage in the annual price review – but also by bending the framework, exploiting its ambiguities and bypassing it. For much of the lifetime of the CAP, common prices have existed only in name, thanks to the system of MCAs. Unequal application of Community preference has encouraged substitution among imports, a development which some producers claim is contrary to the spirit of Community preference; the common financing has been accompanied by national financial measures, some of which nullify the purpose of the CAP.

Monetary compensatory amounts

The monetary basis of the CAP was the agricultural unit of account, an accounting device whose value in terms of gold was fixed in 1962 to equal that of the US dollar.[1] Under the system of fixed parities that obtained in the 1960s the exchange rate between each member state's currency and the unit of account (the 'green rate') was the same as its rate against the dollar.[2] In August 1969 the French franc was devalued against the dollar. The dollar was now worth more in terms of the franc, and the unit of account should have been too. Since common prices were set in units of account, this would have meant an increase in agricultural prices expressed in French francs. To avoid this inflationary effect, France decided to maintain the former rate of exchange between the franc and the unit of account, so that internal French agricultural prices expressed in francs were unchanged. The Council of Ministers agreed to a phased devaluation over two years.

With or without a devaluation of the green franc, prices of exports and imports expressed in francs would have risen because, though agricultural prices were fixed in units of account, proceeds from exports and payments for imports were converted at the new market exchange rate. The difference lay in the relationship between domestic prices and prices of exports and imports: a devaluation of the green rate would mean domestic agricultural prices rising by the same amount as export and import prices; without a devaluation domestic agricultural prices would be unchanged, while export and import prices would rise. Consequently, French producers would find it more profitable to export than to sell on the domestic market.

It was evident that speculators were buying up French cereals and preparing to move them into Germany to sell to intervention agencies there. So that trade would not be distorted, it was agreed to neutralize the difference between the franc price of goods sold in France and to other member states by imposing an export levy. This levy was a monetary compensatory amount (MCA): the difference between the market rate and the green rate for the French franc expressed in percentage terms. Similarly, to maintain at their pre-devaluation level the French franc prices of agricultural imports from Germany, an import subsidy was introduced; and comparable arrangements were applied to trade with non-EEC countries.

Two months later Germany revalued the Deutsche Mark relative to the dollar but, to avoid a fall in internal agricultural prices that would be detrimental to its producers, did not revalue the green rate. This reduced the profitability of agricultural exports relative to sales to home markets because, though the price paid for German agricultural exports was unchanged in terms of other countries' currencies, at the new market exchange rate it was lower in Deutsche Mark terms; and internal Deutsche Mark prices stayed constant. To maintain the profitability of German exports, an export subsidy was introduced, and to maintain import prices at the pre-revaluation Deutsche Mark levels, imports were subjected to a levy. As with the French green rate devaluation, the revaluation of the German green rate was to be phased over two years.

Thus the system of MCAs was set up: negative, involving export levies and import subsidies, for a country whose green rate had not been devalued with its market exchange rate; positive, involving export subsidies and import levies, for a country whose green rate had not been revalued with its market rate. The system of MCAs is not a magic formula for making disparate prices common but a means of influencing the way in which price differentials operate. The capacity to allow green and market rates to diverge gives a member state some control over the real level of agricultural prices within its borders. MCAs ensure that, though real prices differ among member states, each of them faces the same prices in terms of national currency on both its own market and those of all other member states.[3]

Once the French and German market rates had changed to their new parities, they were again fixed, so the difference between them and the respective green rates was fixed and hence MCAs were fixed. MCAs were devised to be temporary instruments to enable orderly adjustment to changes in fixed exchange rates. In 1971, however, the international system of fixed parities broke down, and was replaced by floating exchange rates. This necessitated extending MCAs to other member states and making them variable. Green rates were still fixed in relation to the unit of account, whose gold value continued to be the same as that of the pre-1971 dollar. MCAs were calculated on the basis of the divergence between a currency's green rate and its market rate, each expressed in terms of the US dollar. The MCA system became bewilderingly complex. Market rates were changing constantly, and on each occasion the Commission had to calculate and telex to member states the corresponding changes in MCAs. At one stage the length of the telexes extended to 40 or 50 feet.[4]

New arrangements were introduced in June 1973 to simplify the system. In February the dollar had again been devalued, and subsequently six of the Community's member states set up the 'joint float', confining movements between their currencies to a margin of 2.25 per cent while allowing them to float against all other currencies. Their central rates were fixed not against the dollar but against the IMF's Special Drawing Right, which had a gold value equal to that of the pre-1971 dollar and so to that of the unit of account. The unit of account was linked to the unweighted average value of the joint-float currencies and in effect floated with them. For these currencies with exchange rates fixed against the unit of account, MCAs would vary only with the green rates. The green rates could be set at the annual price-fixing and the MCAs determined for the following year.[5] The three member states whose currencies were to continue floating independently, Ireland, Italy and the UK, would continue to have variable MCAs.[6]

Further efforts to achieve greater monetary order in the Community resulted in the setting up in March 1979 of the European Monetary System (EMS), in which all the member states except the UK participated. The participants established central rates against the European Currency Unit (ECU), whose value was based on a 'basket' of all the member states' currencies, including the pound sterling.[7] The ECU replaced the unit of account, which was valued at 1.21 ECU, and both common agricultural prices and green rates have since been expressed in ECU. Fixed MCAs are calculated using currencies' central rates against the ECU, and hence are fixed except when green rates change. For the pound there continue to be variable MCAs.

MCAs permit some elements of the common pricing system to be retained when divergence among member states' economies, reflected in exchange-rate movements (though sometimes to an exaggerated extent), makes the maintenance of common prices unacceptable. Prices continue to be set in a standard unit of account, so that percentage changes are uniform. At the same time each member state has some leeway in determining the level of agricultural prices as expressed in its national currency (its green rate), and hence the real level of agricultural prices, that is, the quantity of agricultural goods needed to buy a given quantity of non-agricultural goods (the internal terms of trade for agriculture).[8]

The choice of price level affects the allocation of resources and distribution of income within a country, as well as transfers between countries through the budget and through trade. A member state may welcome the opportunity to set its own price level but deplore the way that another member state exercises the same prerogative because of the implications for transfers between them.

The range of choice available to a country depends on the direction in which its currency moves. If a member state's market rate rises and it allows its green rate to follow, then in national currency agricultural prices (fixed in ECU) will fall while other domestic prices initially remain unchanged.[9] There follows a reallocation of resources and a redistribution of income away from agriculture towards the rest of the economy. This can be avoided by not revaluing the green rate with the market rate, in which case there is a positive MCA applied (export subsidy and import levy).[10] Conversely, if a member state's market rate falls and the green rate with it, agricultural prices rise, and resources and income shift towards agriculture from the rest of the economy. This can be avoided by not devaluing the green rate, entailing a negative MCA.

Most countries have wanted to favour agriculture, so those with strong currencies have maintained green rates lower than their market rates, and hence had positive MCAs (Benelux, Germany and since 1980 the UK), and those with weak currencies have maintained parity between green and market rates, and so avoided MCAs (Denmark, Ireland).[11] Three countries have kept green rates higher than their market rates, and hence had negative MCAs (France, Italy and until 1979 the UK). In the case of France this reflected no lack of concern about producers but anxiety about inflation, coupled with willingness to provide farmers with sizable nationally financed subsidies which indirectly compensate for the effect of negative MCAs. For most of the 1970s Italy and the UK had persistently high rates of inflation, and their currencies were under constant downward pressure. The pound's market and green rates parted company almost as soon as the UK joined the Community in 1973. From 1974 to 1979 a Labour government was in power that had no particular obligation to agriculture but was anxious to hold down food prices as part of its 'social contract' with the trade unions, and as a result the internal terms of trade of agriculture were allowed to deteriorate.[12]

The stance adopted by a member state with regard to its green rate may entail transfers between it and other member states through the budget or through trade. Since 1 January 1973 the levies and subsidies associated with MCAs have passed through the FEOGA. Positive MCAs involve export subsidies and import levies; negative MCAs involve export levies and import subsidies. Levies are paid by member states to FEOGA; subsidies by FEOGA to member states. The aggregate effect on the Community budget will affect all member states' budget contributions, that is, if levies amount to more than subsidies, the VAT-based contributions to own resources increase. Whether a member state is a net recipient of, or a net contributor to, MCA transfers depends on the strength of its currency, on the green rate it chooses and on its net trading position in agricultural goods. No member state need be a net contributor on its own account: by keeping its green rate and market rate at par, it can have a nil MCA and so have neither levies nor subsidies. Indirectly, however, its budget contribution is affected by what other member states do.

On budget grounds other member states do not normally object to a member state electing to be a net contributor but do object to a member state electing to be a net recipient. Germany, and until 1979 the UK, illustrated these two cases. Germany, which had an inefficient agricultural sector and a prosperous economy, chose to protect its agriculture at the expense of the rest of the economy. Consequently, it did not revalue the green Mark and, because it was a net importer, became a large contributor of MCA transfers. The UK, which had an efficient agriculture sector and a less prosperous economy, chose to protect agriculture less so as to benefit the rest of the economy. Consequently, it did not devalue the green pound and, because it was a net importer, became a large recipient of MCA transfers.[13]

Whereas Germany did not incur opposition from other member states to its contribution, the UK was under sustained pressure to devalue the green pound and so reduce its MCA receipts. Domestic pressure against the two countries' chosen policies was also asymmetric: the overall strength of Germany's economy brought rising real income, which made it politically easier to maintain relatively high food prices; the overall weakness of the UK's economy, in combination with the chosen policy, yielded declining real income in agriculture, which meant that farmers' demands for devaluation of the green pound could not be indefinitely disregarded.

When it comes to trade flows, the position is reversed. A decision not to accompany a market-rate devaluation with a green-rate devaluation, together with the consequent negative MCAs, means that all agricultural prices stay the same in domestic currency. Devaluation of a green rate means that, in domestic prices, export receipts and import prices are higher and so confers a competitive trading advantage on agriculture. A decision not to revalue the green rate when the market rate is appreciating, and consequent positive MCAs, afford agriculture protection from increased competition, since otherwise revaluation would cause export receipts and import prices to fall in domestic currency and so give competitors a trade advantage. On trade grounds other member states do not object to a member state denying an advantage to its own agriculture but do object to a member state denying an advantage to its competitors' agriculture. Hence negative MCAs are not controversial while positive MCAs are.

France has been greatly upset by Germany's positive MCAs. The export subsidies have encouraged German exports, and their market share has risen, though Germany remains a net importer (*see Table 13*). This prevents France from reaping a trade benefit from the fact that in real terms French franc agricultural prices are lower than Deutsche Mark prices. France has argued that MCAs were intended to aid member states whose currencies were in difficulty, not to advance the interests of those with strong currencies.

The recent history of the UK's MCAs elucidates the contrast between other countries' objections to the budgetary effects of negative MCAs and to the trade effects of positive MCAs. The Labour government's preference for large negative MCAs drew complaints from the Danish government, among others, that the subsidies on goods coming into the UK were a burden on the Community budget. The trade benefit that agricultural exporters to the UK market derived because food prices there were lower than they would otherwise have been was, however, discounted.[14] By 1980 the pound had strengthened to a market rate that was higher than its green rate, and the Conservative government chose not to revalue the green rate. Danish producers then began to complain that the resulting import levy had caused their exports of bacon to decline, and that if the levy were removed they would be able to lower the price and so boost consumption.[15] The transition was described from a different perspective by Mr Hans Kjeldsen, the president of the Danish Agricultural Council, who noted that when the UK had had negative MCAs the National Farmers' Union had opposed divergence between green rates and market rates, but now that it had positive MCAs the NFU defended divergent rates.[16]

France opposed positive MCAs so strongly that it tried to make their abolition a condition for the introduction of the EMS. Eventually Germany agreed to dismantle positive MCAs, but subject to a 'buffer' rule that any reduction in positive MCAs must be accompanied by at least an equal increase in common prices. Since the establishment of the EMS there has been less divergence among member states' currencies, and MCAs have become smaller or disappeared.[17] The exception has been the UK, which has not participated in the EMS. The floating up of the pound resulted in large positive MCAs, which peaked at 18.2 per cent in February 1981. Following the realignment within the EMS at the beginning of October, MCAs were: France, −1.5; Germany, +8.3; Netherlands, +4.3; Italy, −3.9; UK, +3.5; and nil for the other five.

The divergence among member states' economies in the 1970s made it impossible to hold to common agricultural prices. The strains that would have resulted, either for producers or for consumers, would have been too great for some member states to endure. Prices were allowed to diverge, by allowing green rates and market rates to diverge, and MCAs equal to the difference between the two rates were applied to prevent this from causing changes in the volume of trade.

Had MCAs been temporary and small, as originally intended, they would have been less of a problem, but they became permanent and at times very large. In July and August 1973 Italy's negative MCA exceeded 28 per cent and Germany's positive MCA 12 per cent; had each aligned the green rate with the market rate of its currency, Italy's agricultural prices would have risen by 40 per cent relative to those of Germany. A somewhat larger gap developed between the UK and Germany early in 1979. These differentials were larger than the tariffs that existed before the Treaty of Rome was signed.[18]

The application over an extended period of a device inhibiting the trade effects of exchange-rate changes and price divergences implied transfers of resources among countries. Because MCAs were commonly financed, these trade transfers were supplemented (in the case of net agricultural exporters) or countered (in the case of net agricultural importers) by budgetary transfers. These transfers engendered tensions between member states. One manifestation of the tensions was that the annual price negotiations became very prolonged and tortuous. Reductions in MCAs were bartered against larger or smaller increases in common prices or against special concessions, such as the consumers' subsidy for butter, of 8½p per pound, which the UK obtained in 1977. In addition, the complexity of the MCA system created serious administrative problems and provided opportunities for speculation by large traders, to the detriment of producers, consumers and small traders.

The size and duration of MCAs perturbed the Commission. In 1975 it acknowledged that they had helped to keep the CAP operating during the transition from fixed to floating exchange rates. They could still serve 'to prevent short-term fluctuations in exchange rates from instantaneously affecting agricultural prices expressed in national currencies'. There should, however, be rules and procedures to ensure that changes in MCAs were 'appropriate'. It was unacceptable that MCAs 'constitute factors disrupting the unity of the agricultural market and generating distortions of competition'.[19]

Constraints were not placed on MCAs, though the adoption of the ECU as a unit of account has brought more harmony into the relationship between green and market rates. Since 1980 divergence among member states' inflation rates has tended to diminish, but it is likely to grow again, especially in view of the prospective enlargement of the Community to twelve members. Experience since 1969 amply demonstrates that common prices pose major problems when inflation rates diverge: if common prices are maintained, individual economies come under intolerable strain; if national agricultural price levels diverge while a semblance of common prices is retained, serious tensions arise between member states.

Ambiguities of Community preference

Unlike common prices, Community preference has been extensively applied since the CAP came into being. The intention is that member states should import a product from another member state rather than from a third country. It has been pursued through the variable import levy, which ensures that prices for goods produced in the Community are lower than prices for the same goods imported from outside the Community. This protection, combined with other factors, has encouraged Community production to increase and to replace imports. A low level of protection, however, is applied to imports of products that are not produced in the Community. To the extent that such products can substitute for imports subject to the higher level of protection, they tend to replace them and also to replace domestic production, which may then have to find export outlets.

The most important instance relates to products used for animal fodder. Livestock rearers, encouraged by the CAP, have expanded production by introducing more intensive farming methods. These have entailed switching from traditional types of fodder, which are forage crops (grass, forage maize) and cereals (common wheat, barley), to low-cost feed systems that rely on vegetable protein products, notably soya. The Community is only 20 per cent self-sufficient in such products, and soya is its largest single agricultural import, accounting for almost half of its large trade deficit in agricultural products with the United States.

Animal feed compounds are produced from soya or other vegetable proteins and cereals, but the cereal content can be largely replaced by other products. These cereal substitutes include manioc, brans and maize gluten feed, which are imported at low or zero rates of duty. They have increasingly displaced both imported cereals (maize) and cereals produced in the Community (common wheat and barley). In the Netherlands, the cereal content of animal feed compounds is now 20 per cent or less.

In the context of the CAP this issue is complex because it opposes farmers employing different methods of production (e.g. dairy farmers using pasture against those using compounds); farmers engaged in different types of production (livestock against cereals); and member states, since particular methods and types of production are often concentrated in particular countries. It also carries implications for the budget: on the revenue side because imported substitutes mean lost receipts from the variable levy on imported cereals; and on the expenditure side because of the cost of disposing of cereals produced in the

Community that are replaced by imported substitutes.

France opposes these imports on several grounds: they contravene Community preference and should be subject to a duty that would equate their price inside the Community to that of imported cereals; proximity to the ports of Rotterdam and Hamburg gives farmers in the Netherlands and Germany cheaper access to imported substitutes; and, last, the CAP was intended to protect farms of a family character, not those organized like factories, which are held responsible for surplus production, particularly dairy. The response of other member states is that to change the treatment of these imports would be to upset existing trade, and that intensive methods enable low-cost efficient production, which is an objective of the CAP. This argument is made emphatically in the Netherlands, where it is also said that widespread use of cattle compounds reflects, not the proximity of Rotterdam, but the competence of Dutch compound manufacturers. In the Netherlands and Denmark, the point is made that a large part of the recent increase in the Community's dairy production has occurred in France.

Under GATT regulations the import duty for soya (zero per cent), manioc (6 per cent) and maize gluten feed (zero per cent) can be changed only after consultation with interested parties with a view to compensation. The Commission has acted directly on manioc by securing agreement from Thailand, the largest supplier to date, to restrict imports to about 5m tonnes a year, against a peak of 6m in 1978. Any further limitation would be firmly resisted by Germany and the Netherlands, which are the largest importers of manioc. Furthermore, the reduction in manioc imports has apparently been made good by imports of other substitutes and not of cereals produced in the Community.

The view taken by the Commission is that imports of competing products represent a breach of Community preference rather than a symptom of the high degree of protection that it implies. In December 1980, the Commission indicated that it would be proposing measures that would 'arrest the excessive rise in imports of these substitutes', and added: 'It is unjustifiable to criticize the operation of the CAP while leaving the door completely open to competing products for political or other reasons.'[20] Nevertheless, as long as protection stays high, the problem will not be easily resolved.

National aids

Community preference was intended to ward off any threat to the unified market from outside the Community, and common financing was to safeguard it from within by making common prices acceptable to member states whose prices had previously been lower. While common financing of price support and export restitutions has been directed towards reinforcing the unified market, member states have spent even larger amounts of national finance on their individual agricultural sectors. The Commission records a wide range of financial aids to agriculture: research, training and advisory services; production assistance encompassing structural and technical measures, income support, cheap credit and subsidized energy prices; marketing and processing; consumer subsidies; income-tax relief; and social security contributions (*see Table 8*).

The total sums involved differ sizably among member states, as do the proportions of the total devoted to various items. The Commission notes that this reflects differences among member states regarding the goals of agricultural policy and the economic and social constitution of farming. It concludes that 'The largest sums are not always being spent in those regions of the Community which have the greatest need of restructuring and adaptation.' This suggests that national financing tends to create rather than remove distortions. It is difficult to identify distortions, however, because the data supplied by member states are based on disparate definitions, and are also incomplete and inaccurate.[21]

Member states are required to give advance notice to the Commission of measures that could affect markets and prices so that it can decide whether to approve them, but this procedure is often not followed. In the summer of 1980 the Commission published a list of 51 illegal aids being applied by member states, of which 39 were in France. Later that year the French government announced further aids, valued at £200m, without notifying the Commission. Seven months and a change of government later, the Commission was still awaiting an explanation. It offered to drop its threat to take the case to the European Court of Justice if France would phase out illegal aids. In the past, however, France has not been perturbed by adverse decisions of the Court. The last Minister of Agriculture, M. Pierre Méhaignerie, acknowledging two judgements against him, remarked, 'But I am still well, I still breathe. British farmers have often wished that their ministers were as robust in their attitudes.'[22]

Despite opposition from the Commission, acting both to defend the Treaty and to assert its authority, member governments have pursued diverse national policy objectives. The lack of convergence stems in part from factors beyond the scope of the CAP but chiefly from the way in which the CAP was set up. Common prices were set high enough that no member state's agriculture had to adjust radically, and none was inhibited in continuing to pursue its national policy. Moreover, in most cases member states wanted to shield agriculture from the effects of relative decline. The CAP helped them to do this and partly to disguise the costs for the rest of the economy of doing so.

6 Costs and benefits

The costs and benefits of the CAP to the Community arise in several ways: it affects the allocation of resources and hence the total income of the Community; it redistributes income among individuals; and it redistributes income among member states, a process partly reflected in balance-of-payments flows between them. It also generates non-marketed costs and benefits; such benefits include the protection of the rural environment. In addition, the CAP entails costs and benefits for the rest of the world.

Allocation of resources

In theory the most efficient allocation of resources in a competitive market is achieved when the prices for all products are at their equilibrium level, where supply is equal to demand; then the value that society places on additional production is equal to the cost of producing it. At price levels above equilibrium, supply exceeds demand. Left to free-market forces, the price falls until it reaches equilibrium. As the price falls, producers with higher costs cease to produce, and there is a shift of resources to other products whose prices are above their equilibrium levels. Failure to move to this more efficient allocation entails a loss to the whole economy. What happens in practice is different because not all the conditions of a competitive market are fulfilled, and because society is concerned about income distribution as well as total income, and governments may intervene on either count.

The fundamental purpose of the CAP was to include agriculture in the European Economic Community. This meant not only 'that the obstacles to the free movement of agricultural products must be removed. More than this, it means that production must be located according to the principle of the optimum allocation of resources and the need for specialization foreseen in Article 43 of the EEC Treaty. Accordingly, it implies that, in the context of the creation of a large market ..., there should be a division of labour reflecting the comparative advantages of widely differing areas.'[1] In other words, a unified market would bring an efficient allocation of resources at Community, rather than national, level. Given the special character of agriculture and the consequent extensive government intervention that already existed at national level, it would be necessary to intervene at Community level to ensure that the unified market operated effectively. This was the reason for establishing a single set of prices that would determine the actions of producers and consumers throughout the Community. Production would then be encouraged to expand in low-cost areas and to contract in high-cost areas. Specialization within a larger market would increase total income to the benefit of both producers and consumers.

In the event, though there has been some specialization at Community level, it has not occurred on the scale that was envisaged. Some telling evidence that it has been far from complete is the fact that France, a country which might have been expected to hold a comparative advantage in agriculture, has not increased its share in the total agricultural production of the Community. One explanation for the limited results is that not all the obstacles to the free movement of agricultural products have been removed. MCAs have caused real prices to differ; national policy measures have also caused distortions, though they sometimes cancel one another out. There have also been technical barriers, such as differences in veterinary regulations, though some have been lowered as a result of efforts to achieve greater harmonization.[2]

Agricultural trade among member states, however, has expanded both absolutely and till lately in relation to their trade with the rest of the world (*see Table 6*). That this expansion has not led to greater specialization is due to the high level of prices and to inadequate price-competitiveness. It was intended that prices should fluctuate between the intervention and the threshold levels, but because these levels have been high, and there has been excess production, prices have generally remained close to their intervention level. The CAP has involved administering prices, through internal price support and Community preference, with the primary object of maintaining farm income rather than improving resource allocation. Instead of the wider market facilitating a division of labour that resulted in a more efficient allocation of resources and increased income, resources have been retained in agriculture, where they are less productive than they would be if they were employed in another sector, and there has been a loss of potential income. An indication, though not a measure, of this loss is the fact that the Community produces more than it can sell at the price it has set. In view of present levels of unemployment, however, perhaps it is better to keep labour underemployed in agriculture than to reallocate it to uses that might be more efficient in theory but are non-existent in practice.

Income distribution

The rationale of the way in which price policy has been applied is that the loss of income caused by an inefficient allocation of resources is justified by gains in terms of a more desirable distribution of income. Income is transferred to farmers from consumers, who pay higher prices than would be needed to ensure the level of consumption they desire, and from all taxpayers, who finance the disposal of that part of production for which there is no demand at the price set by the Community. It is not clear that these transfers have brought about a more equitable distribution of income, since the richest farmers appear to have benefited most at the expense of the poorest consumers.

The Commission has acknowledged that the CAP's market organizations 'work to the advantage of the largest producers, who already have the most favourable production structures', and noted that there was opposition to 'public money being used, for the most part to support the incomes of the richest farmers'.[3] The document went on to refer to a related criticism, which was that the CAP had been of more assistance to regions that were already rich than to the least-favoured regions. This partly reflected differences in natural resources and in structure that predated the Community. It had to be recognized, however, that there were large regional disparities among regions and, worse still, that these had in most cases widened during the 1970s.[4] The price policy benefited the richer regions disproportionately because it favoured northern products and better-off producers, both of which were concentrated in those regions. A very close correlation existed between a region's agricultural income and the support it received. On a base of 100 for average expenditure per labour unit in the Community, the index was above 150 for most regions in the Paris basin, Belgium, north Germany, the Netherlands and Denmark; generally below 50 in one out of three regions in Italy; and below 80 in most other Italian regions, mountain regions and south-west France.

While it has ensured that within the farm sector proportionately more income has been transferred to those who have least need, among consumers the CAP has resulted in proportionately more income being transferred from those least able to afford it. Because food is a basic necessity, low-income households devote a larger part of their expenditure to it than do high-income households. In the UK in 1976, for example, among households with children, those with low incomes spent 34 per cent of their budget on food and those with high incomes 21 per cent.[5] The average food expenditure of low-income households with children was also higher in absolute terms than that of high-income households without children. Furthermore, low-income countries devote a larger part of their expenditure to food. In 1978 the proportion for all households ranged from 15.6 per cent in Germany to 29.2 per cent in Italy.[6] Hence the poorer consumers in each member state, and consumers in general in the poorer member states (notably Ireland and Italy), have contributed proportionately and even absolutely more of the income transferred to farmers.

The generally progressive orientation of national tax systems means that taxpayers' contributions to farm income are more equitably based than those of consumers, though, since tax systems differ substantially, and since again no distinction is made between richer and poorer member states, taxpayers in one part of the Community pay more than taxpayers with comparable incomes elsewhere.

Transfers between member states

Because of the basic framework of the CAP, transfers to farmers from taxpayers and consumers generate balance-of-payments flows between member states. Common financing means that the cost of supporting prices and disposing of surplus production is a charge not on national exchequers but on the Community budget, which is financed from own resources. Community preference means that instead of paying the world price for imports a member state pays the price set by the Community. For an import from a third country this comprises the world price plus the variable import levy; for an import from another member state the Community price goes in full to that member state. In the first case, the revenue from the levy appears in the importing country's contribution to the Community's own resources; in the second case, there is in effect a direct transfer (a 'trade transfer') from the importing to the exporting member state equivalent to the levy. For an exporter, the price received for an export to a third country may include an export refund paid from the Community budget, while the price for an export to another member state includes a transfer.

Various attempts have been made to quantify the transfer effects of the CAP. In the UK in recent years, research has been prompted by the country's very large net contribution to the Community budget. This problem has tended to focus attention on financial flows, which are comparatively straightforward to calculate. Figures showing member states' receipts from FEOGA are published in its financial reports. Member states contribute to the budget as a whole rather than to individual elements of it; the usual assumption is that the proportion of a member state's contribution that goes to FEOGA is equal to the share of FEOGA in the total budget.[7]

Financial transfers alone, however, understate the full impact of the CAP on the balances of payments of member states, and are also a misleading indicator in that the more a country concentrates its trade within the Community, rather than within the rest of the world, the less the financial transfers will be, although the effective transfer may be the same. A complete picture requires the inclusion of trade transfers, but these are more difficult to calculate. Such estimates require assumptions about the policies that member states would apply if there were no CAP (the price level they would set and how they would support it) and the implications for world prices.

The approach used by the UK Ministry of Agriculture is to assume that member states would continue to apply all CAP price levels and support mechanisms but without common financing or Community preference. In the absence of common financing, import levies and export restitutions would continue to apply to trade with third countries, but they would be payments to or charges on national exchequers rather than the Community budget. This effect is incorporated in the financial transfers. In the absence of Community preference, levies and restitutions would also apply to trade among member states. As a policy alternative this hypothetical situation is neither feasible nor desirable, but as a method of analysis it has several advantages: no estimate need be made of the impact of changed policies on the direction of trade or on world prices, and the variable import levy can be used as a measure of the trade transfers.[8] The results of the Ministry's calculations for 1978 and 1979 are shown in the table below.

The Ministry of Agriculture's method is intended to pick out the effects of common financing and Community preference, not to represent a realistic policy option. It is improbable that a set of national policies

Estimated balance-of-payments costs and benefits arising from the CAP (£ million)

	1978			1979		
	Transfers through FEOGA budget	Est. trade transfers	Est. total cost of CAP	Transfers through FEOGA budget	Est. trade transfers	Est. total cost of CAP
Germany	122	434	556	465	125	590
France	−41	−575	−616	−255	−600	−850
Italy	344	588	932	−4	700	700
Netherlands	−241	−605	−846	−329	−325	−650
B-Lux	−33	54	21	−49	300	250
UK	673	110	783	882	225	1110
Ireland	−343	−184	−527	−339	−275	−610
Denmark	−408	−275	−683	−336	−375	−710

Note: The method underlying these calculations is described in GES Working Paper No. 27 (see note 8). The 'total cost' columns do not sum to zero for technical reasons explained in paragraphs 38 and 39.
Source: Nineteenth Report of the Select Committee on the European Communities of the House of Lords, Session 1980/1, vol. 2 (London: HMSO, 1981), p. 194.

would closely resemble the CAP. For some member states, notably Denmark and Ireland, the amount of commonly financed price support that their producers receive under the CAP would be too great a burden if they had to finance it nationally. Other member states, such as the UK, might prefer to protect their producers by producer subsidies instead of import levies. Also, without the CAP the divergence among member states' price levels would probably be still greater. Research undertaken at the Institute for Fiscal Studies (IFS) uses the assumption that, without the CAP, trade among member states would take place at world prices.[9] Those world prices would depend chiefly on how aggregate supply and demand would differ from the present situation, but also on some of the peculiar factors that influence agricultural prices in world trade.[10] A calculation of this sort is inevitably somewhat speculative, but detailed information about the market for each individual product suggests that in many cases world prices might remain close to present levels.

The IFS research attempts to capture the effects of the price level and type of support applied by the CAP, as well as those of common financing and Community preference, and so to arrive at a comprehensive assessment for each member state of gains and losses, comprising not only financial and trade transfers but also the effects on resource allocation. Five types of flows are quantified:

(1) losses to consumers from higher prices (domestic consumption multiplied by the difference between domestic and world prices);

(2) losses to consumers from the reduction in demand (consumption at world prices less consumption at domestic prices);

(3) gains to producers from higher prices (domestic production multiplied by the difference between domestic and world prices);

(4) additional costs incurred by producers of output that would not be produced at world prices (production at domestic prices less production at world prices); and

(5) net budgetary contribution to agricultural support derived from taxes on non-agricultural products.[11]

Item 2 occurs because higher prices discourage consumption and so result in a loss to consumers that is not compensated by a gain to producers. In the case of item 4, producers gain less from additional output induced by higher prices than from output at world prices because the production cost of additional output is higher. Both item 2 and item 4 require estimates of how European demand and supply have responded to the increased prices which result from the CAP. These raise several practical difficulties. The results are shown in the table below. The net loss to the Community of £4.1 billion derives from three major sources: items 2 and 4 and the cost of storage. After allowance has been made for a number of smaller items, there is a shortfall of £900m between producer receipts and consumer and taxpayer payments, which is explained by leakages and errors.

Although the results of the Ministry of Agriculture and the IFS are not directly comparable, they point to broadly similar conclusions. Both show Germany, Italy and the UK to be the main contributors, and Ireland, Denmark and the Netherlands the chief beneficiaries. This indicates a close correlation between the extent to which a member state benefits from the CAP and its level of self-sufficiency in agricultural products. As the next table shows, it is difficult to discern any pattern with regard

Transfers between member states, 1978 (£m)

Country	Consumer loss*	Producer gain†	Budgetary contribution	Total effect on resources
Germany	4598	4035	1177	−1740
France	3167	3642	761	−286
Italy	3413	2257	386	−1541
Netherlands	892	1403	305	+206
Belgium	725	680	226	−259
United Kingdom	1787	1148	731	−1370
Ireland	175	408	32	+201
Denmark	291	713	117	+324
Other subsidies and restitutions‡	−7		−380	
Total	15,041*	14,286†	3357	−4112

* After allowing for subsidies.
† Includes Guidance Section payments.
‡ Subsidies not allocated to countries are under 'Consumer loss', and restitutions and subsidies on products not covered are under 'Budgetary contribution'.
Source: C. N. Morris, 'The Common Agricultural Policy', *Fiscal Studies*, vol. 1, no. 2 (1980), p. 28.

Effects of transfers on member states' economies, 1978

Country	Consumer and Taxpayer loss	Approximate producer gain per person in agriculture	Change in resources per capita	Change in resources as % GDP
	(£ p.a.)	(£ p.a.)	(£ p.a.)	
Germany	93.4	2400	−28.2	−0.53
France	74.5	1800	−5.4	−0.12
Italy	68.1	700	−27.6	−1.26
Netherlands	87.4	4900	+15.0	+0.31
Belgium	93.2	5100	−25.4	−0.50
United Kingdom	45.0	1700	−24.5	−0.86
Ireland	66.8	1700	+64.8	+3.24
Denmark	81.6	3200	+64.8	+1.15
EUR-9	71.2	1700	−15.9	−0.41

Source: Morris, 'The CAP', p.29.

to per capita income. Ireland, the poorest country in the Community, gains most on a per capita basis, but Denmark and the Netherlands are high-income countries and also gain, while Italy and the UK are low-income countries and lose. In terms of the effect on GDP, the smaller countries gain proportionately more. For Ireland the balance-of-payments effect calculated by the Ministry represents 7–8 per cent of GDP.

Evidence has been presented which suggests that the operation of the CAP results in a sizable loss to the Community as a whole; that its effects on income distribution are skewed to the detriment of poor consumers and to the advantage of rich producers; and that it causes transfers from member states that are net importers to those that are net exporters. Such evidence is not readily accepted by those groups and member states that gain from the CAP. They counter it by citing non-economic benefits such as protection of the environment and a traditional lifestyle in rural areas, the maintenance of law and order in regions with an obstreperous agricultural population, and strategic supply security. These benefits are difficult to quantify, but the order of magnitude of the quantifiable losses indicated above suggests it is unlikely that they could significantly affect the overall negative balance sheet.

Impact on the world market

Although analysis of the costs and benefits of the CAP has chiefly concerned transfers between groups and countries within the Community, attention has also been drawn to its repercussions on the world market. Whereas the CAP was devised to minimize the impact of world market conditions on the Community's internal market, the sheer size of the Community's trade with the rest of the world inevitably implies that the CAP has an impact on the world market. The Community is the world's largest importer and second largest exporter (after the United States) of agricultural products.

The high common prices established by the CAP somewhat dampened demand in the Community while encouraging production to expand. The Community's demand from the world market declined and, as it became more self-sufficient, it increasingly sought export markets in the rest of the world. Third countries found themselves first squeezed out of the Community's market and then competing with the Community in other markets.

The protection provided by the CAP tends to depress world prices: import levies increase Community, and hence total world, production, while export restitutions enable the Community to sell on the world market at low prices. Moreover, the variable nature of the import levy provided for by the CAP increases the instability of world prices. The purpose of the levy is to ensure that prices of goods imported into the Community remain constant: any change in world prices is counterbalanced by a change in the levy so that internal prices are unchanged. The variable levy is unique in blocking the transmission of disturbances in the world market.[12] *Ad valorem* or specific tariffs allow domestic prices to vary with world prices, and the resulting variations in domestic supply and demand absorb part of the disturbances in the world market. They also allow a decline in domestic supply, for example following a poor harvest, to be absorbed partly by the domestic market through higher prices. Even a fixed import quota permits this to happen. The variable levy rules out all these effects. Only on the rare occasions when shortages cause world prices to rise above Community prices is some transmission of disturbances possible. Then, however, the variable import levy becomes a variable export tax that restricts exports at a time of world scarcity, so exacerbating instability again.

The insulation of part of the world market from disturbances amplifies the disturbances in the rest of the world market. Since world supply and demand are slow to respond to price movements, variations in net Community supply and demand, even though these may be a small fraction of world production, result in sizable fluctuations in world prices. Although exporting countries are not necessarily harmed by unstable prices, they usually prefer stability. Importing countries are more likely to suffer, particularly if they are poor countries that encounter extreme hardship when prices are high. In so far as it lowers long-run average world prices, the CAP benefits importing countries to the detriment of exporting countries.

It is this last aspect that has created most opposition to the CAP outside the Community. Australia and New Zealand, in particular, complain of increased competition from subsidized Community exports of meat to Eastern Europe, North Africa and the Middle and Far East. Australia is also concerned about exports of cereals, sugar and canned fruit. Some of these apprehensions have been echoed by the United States, Argentina and Brazil. Furthermore, efforts by established suppliers to replace markets lost to the Community have knock-on effects, as they in turn sell at low prices that put pressure on other exporting countries whose foothold in agricultural trade is less firm.

Australia has pressed vigorously within the GATT for modifications to the Community's export subsidies, notably for sugar. In March 1981 a GATT working party reported that the Community's subsidized exports were hurting efficient exporters, such as Australia, Brazil, Cuba and the Dominican Republic. In September the GATT Council implicitly rejected the Community's claim that its new sugar regime conformed with the GATT, and set up a broader-based working party to report by March 1982. Australia's deputy prime minister has urged that an alliance of food-producing nations be formed to exert strong moral pressure on the Community to change its policy. Opposition to the CAP from the United States was muted during the Carter administration but is now being renewed. The Reagan administration has informed the Community that it will pursue an aggressive free-market policy and, in particular, will resist encroachments on its traditional markets from subsidized exports of wheat from the Community.[13]

Within the Community the costs and benefits that the CAP generates in the rest of the world are of secondary importance. The CAP was formulated as an internal policy. Its treatment of imports was a consequence of its purpose of increasing agricultural production within the Community; its treatment of exports derived from the need to dispose of its surplus production. To consider repercussions on the rest of the world was not within the CAP's terms of reference. They cannot, however, be ignored with impunity. Like other trading countries, the Community has an interest in avoiding disruption of the international trading system. This, as the Commission has said, requires give and take on all sides.

Relations with Australia have indicated how the CAP's external implications can rebound on the Community. In 1980 proposals to establish a CAP regime for sheepmeat met with a threat to divert up to A $1 billion in Australian government purchases from EEC countries. This was withdrawn after safeguards were written into the regime to protect established sheepmeat producers. After visiting Australia and New Zealand in April 1980, the German minister of defence stressed that these countries' ability to play an effective military role in their region depended not least on their earnings from agricultural exports to the Community. He also noted that Europe would need Australia's raw materials and energy resources over the next decade. Clearly Australia is better placed than most countries to influence the Community, but its case has a general application: the CAP has an impact on the economies of other countries and hence on their capacity to import from the Community, as well as on their overall relations with the Community.

The inadequate fulfilment of the CAP's objectives and the substantial costs that it has entailed have prompted numerous proposals for changing it. The European Commission, the European Parliament, national governments and ministries, independent commissions, political parties and individual politicians, research institutes, academics, journalists and interest groups (most of them from the farm sector but some representing industry, commerce, trade unions or consumers) have contributed to a steady stream of material analysing and frequently prescribing for the CAP. Nor has this output been confined to the Community: the CAP has received attention also from international organizations and from non-EEC countries.[14] A number of proposals are now being considered with a view to curbing the budgetary cost of the CAP, and will be discussed in the next chapter.

7 Budget reform

Various factors have recently begun to exert pressure on the budget. Since the CAP accounts for by far the largest part of the Community budget, changes in budgetary arrangements will entail changes in the CAP. Because it is pressure on the budget that has prompted active consideration of possible revisions to the CAP, the proposals are generally conceived in the context of relieving that pressure. Some of the suggested ways of doing this would effectively mean shifting the costs of the CAP from the Community budget to consumers, to national budgets or to third countries. They would leave the CAP operating essentially as at present and would have little effect on its overall cost. Others would imply more radical reform that would reduce both budget and non-budget costs.

Pressures

Throughout the history of the Community some of the fiercest struggles among member states have been about finance. At the outset each part of Community activity was separately financed, the revenue coming from national exchequers. Contributions were shared among member states, on a percentage basis set out in the Treaty, which reflected their ability to pay and their involvement in a particular area of policy.

In 1965 the Commission put forward proposals for the future financing of the CAP. It suggested that the Community should implement Treaty commitments to acquire direct revenue in the form of customs duties and agricultural import levies. This revenue was expected to exceed expenditure requirements, and the surplus would be redistributed among member states so as to promote an equitable sharing of burdens. The French government opposed this, as well as other items in the Commission's financial package, and for six months did not participate in Community institutions. As a result, revenue continued to come from direct national contributions, though from 1967 FEOGA received 90 per cent of agricultural import levies and financed directly the whole of guarantee expenditure. It still operated as a clearing-house, however, member states seeking reimbursement of sums they had already paid out.

The ending of the transitional period of the European Economic Community in 1970 was followed by changes in financial arrangements. In 1971 the scope of the general budget was extended to most of the specific areas of expenditure, including FEOGA, which was the largest single item. Member states were to receive advances based on estimates of their expenditure on the CAP. The budget was to become steadily less dependent on national contributions for its resources. It was to draw on all agricultural import levies and an increasing proportion of customs duties, reaching 100 per cent in 1975. In the same year contributions from national exchequers were to be replaced by an arrangement whereby a proportion of the national receipts from value added tax (VAT) became Community property. It was assumed that by 1975 the requisite harmonization of member states' tax bases would have been achieved, but in the event VAT-based contributions were implemented only from 1979.[1]

From the late 1960s the German government began to complain about the size of its net contribution to Community finances. It was also clear that Italy received proportionately less than other member states. German grievances were discounted by other member states because of the strong and expanding German economy, while Italy's situation was ascribed to a low take-up resulting from factors such as administrative and legislative difficulties.

Net contributions of individual member states received renewed attention during the negotiations that preceded the UK's accession to the Community in 1973. Cost was a major issue in the domestic political debate about membership. The UK expected the size of its gross contributions to be large because it was a substantial net importer of agricultural products, and because much of its trade, both agricultural and non-agricultural, was with third countries and so would become subject to Community levies and duties. Its receipts, however, would be small because the major part of the budget was spent on agriculture, and the UK had only a small agricultural sector.

Other member governments and the Commission pointed out that once the UK was a member, it would trade increasingly with the rest of the Community, and that VAT, which reflected a member state's overall level of economic activity, was expected to account for a larger proportion of budget revenue. On the expenditure side, new policies were expected to be developed in the regional, social and industrial fields that would reduce agriculture's share of the budget to 60 per cent or even 40 per cent. To help dispel the UK's apprehensions, the original member states agreed that if in the future 'unacceptable situations' arose, 'the very survival of the Community would demand that the Institutions find equitable solutions'.[2] When the terms of the UK's entry were renegotiated by the Labour government in 1975, a more concrete reassurance was given in the form of the 'financial mechanism'. This was a formula providing that if an 'unacceptable situation' occurred, in which a member state's economy was 'forced to bear a disproportionate burden in the financing of the Community budget', the member state should, subject to certain conditions, be entitled to a partial refund of its gross contributions.

The impact of the Community's budgetary arrangements on the UK was delayed by the transitional phase of membership. Not until 1980 was the UK to pay its contribution in full. By early 1979, however, it was evident that the UK was overtaking Germany as the largest net contributor (*see Table 4*). Although there had been a sizable shift in the direction of the UK's trade towards the Community, its gross contribution remained large; its receipts were still small because agriculture continued to account for some 70 per cent of Community expenditure. The financial mechanism did not bring relief because, while the UK met the economic conditions (per capita GNP less than 85 per cent of the Community average, and growth rate of per capita GNP less than 120 per cent of the Community average), it was prevented from receiving any benefit by other conditions (mainly that a member state's share of *gross* contributions must exceed its share of Community GNP by more than 10 per cent).

Consequently, the Labour government and, after May 1979, the Conservative government began to insist that further revisions were needed in order to achieve a reduction in the UK's net contribution to the budget. The UK's position was that, though the budget did not accurately reflect the full economic costs and benefits of the Community, it was unfair that a member state should make a disproportionate contribution, particularly if the member state was relatively poor. The debate proceeded at several levels. The question of principle was what role, if any, equity should play in determining the distribution of net contributions to the budget. In practical terms this became an argument about how much money the UK should get back, and hence how much more other member states would have to pay. Efforts were made to obtain in return concessions from the UK in other matters, including the 1980 price review, the proposed sheepmeat regime, fisheries policy, North Sea oil and UK participation in the EMS. Since the UK's situation arose in part because of the dominant position of the CAP in Community expenditure, it focused attention on the underlying issue of the Community's failure to develop other common policies and other major fields of expenditure, and led to proposals to 'restructure' the budget in favour of other items of expenditure. The British problem also reflected the economic divergence among member states, which had begun to emerge after the recession of the mid-1970s and had received much attention during the discussions about setting up the EMS in 1978.

After tough and prolonged negotiations, agreement was reached at the end of May 1980 on a complicated formula for reducing the UK's budget contribution. About one-third of the amount was to be obtained as a result of adaptations to the financial mechanism which were to function automatically up to the end of 1982. The other two-thirds were to come from supplementary measures financed by the Community that would aim to improve the economic performance of the UK through the development of economic and social infrastructure and the exploitation of coal resources. These measures could take several years to complete but could be initiated only up to the end of 1981.[3] For the longer run the Community pledged to find more lasting means of resolving the problem. The Commission was given a mandate to examine the development of Community policies with a view to proposing by the end of June 1981 structural changes in the budget that would prevent the recurrence of 'unacceptable situations'.

Without the May 1980 budget agreement, the UK in 1980 would have contributed 20.5 per cent of budget revenue and received 8.5 per cent of budget expenditure, while its share of GNP was 16.0 per cent. The problem stems partly from a disproportionately large contribution, but more from disproportionately small receipts. These reflect the fact that about 65 per cent of the Community's budget is spent on agricultural price guarantees, and of this amount only 5 per cent goes to the UK. To restructure budget expenditure in a way that lowered the UK's net contribution would thus require a substantial reduction in the proportion spent on agriculture.

As well as the structure of the budget, the overall size of the budget is beginning to generate problems. The system of 'own resources' for the Community budget which was drawn up in 1970 comprised agricultural levies, customs duties and a VAT element. It was agreed that this last would be the proceeds of a flat rate of up to 1 per cent on all transactions within the harmonized VAT base.[4] By the time the system came into force in 1979, it was evident that the expenditure required to meet commitments under present policies was approaching the 1 per cent VAT limit on own resources. The more self-sufficient the Community becomes in agricultural products, the more problematic are the existing financial arrangements of the CAP. Revenue from import levies declines relative to the expenditure needed to dispose of excess production. At one stage it seemed that the VAT limit would be reached before the end of 1981. Recently expenditure has been increasing more slowly, mainly because a rise in world prices has reduced the amount by which the Community has to subsidize its agricultural exports to bring them down to the world price level. If present trends continue, it will be 1983 before expenditure exceeds the own-resources ceiling.

Expenditure in excess of the ceiling will clearly be necessary when Spain and Portugal join the Community, which is due to be in January 1984. The cost of supporting southern products, notably olive oil, will rise and will be only partially offset by the reduction in the cost of supporting those northern products of which the two countries are net importers. Because for northern products they are high-cost producers, it is uncertain what effect the application of CAP price support will have on production.

Enlargement of the Community to twelve member states is already creating pressures for new expenditure. Italian and French producers are anxious about the effects that enlargement will have on the competitiveness of their Mediterranean products, and will continue to seek additional support for them before Spain and Portugal are admitted. The package of structural measures for the Mediterranean regions introduced in 1978 was a response to their concerns. It is expected that the inclusion of Spain will add substantial weight and negotiating skill in support of the interests of producers of Mediterranean products. Once the number of Mediterranean member states is increased, there will be growing pressure for the CAP to treat southern products in the same way as northern products.

Although restructuring is the issue that has to be tackled first, the approach to it will be influenced by the fact that the other two budget issues, the own-resources ceiling and enlargement, are in the offing. The restructuring exercise is made more difficult by the very limited scope for increasing total expenditure. Until agreement has been reached on restructuring, however, it is unlikely that some member governments would consider increasing revenue. There is also a link between restructuring and enlargement, since under the present system Portugal would be a net contributor to the budget despite being the poorest member of the Community.

Various approaches to restructuring have been suggested. Gross contributions could be redistributed by replacing or altering the own-resources system, for example, by an oil-import tax. Alternatively there could be direct adjustment of member states' net contributions, similar in operation to the financial mechanism. On the expenditure side, attention has been directed towards lowering the proportion taken up by the CAP. For the CAP, restructuring and the other budget issues all point in the same direction: the need to reduce the share of agriculture in total spending, the imminent constraint on revenue, and the prospect that after enlargement the CAP will inevitably cost more, all create pressure for curbing the budget costs of the CAP.

Even before the Commission was given its mandate to propose ways of restructuring the budget, those opposed to curbing the budget costs of the CAP had begun to advance arguments to demonstrate that the proportion of budget expenditure attributable to the CAP was smaller than usually supposed. FEOGA, it is said, is being made to pay for other Community policies. Reference is made to a study undertaken by COPA in February 1980 which showed that expenditure on food aid, and the revenue forgone on account of imports of agricultural goods under preferential agreements, added up to ECU 1.9 billion.[5] These budgetary costs derive from the Community's aid and foreign policies, and so should appear under those headings in the budget. In addition, MCAs are blamed on the inadequacies of the Community's monetary policy, so it is claimed they should not be charged to agriculture. If the budget is redrawn along these lines, expenditure on the CAP appears to amount to only 60 per cent of the budget, and if revenue from levies and duties on agricultural imports is deducted from expenditures, the figure falls below 50 per cent. Although some of these steps are highly questionable, a more defensible procedure reaches a figure around 55 per cent (*see Chapter 6, note 11*).

The most serious efforts to change budget headings have been directed at sugar imported under the Lomé Convention and at food aid. Food aid was conceived as a means of helping to dispose of the Community's excess production, since it is cheaper to give food away than to pay for storing it. Other exporting countries criticize food aid on the grounds that it is in practice dumping, and some third world importing countries on the grounds that it upsets their domestic markets, is nutritionally unsuitable and is sporadic. It is unlikely that food aid or any other item will be transferred to another heading, partly because by now this would be politically too controversial, but mainly because it would affect neither the total cost of the budget nor the distribution of net contributions among member states.

Arguments are also put forward to defend the absolute size of agricultural expenditure. The budgetary cost of the CAP is still only 0.5 per cent of the Community's GDP, though up from 0.35 per cent in 1976. If national aids are included, the figure for spending on agricultural policy rises to 1.5 per cent, which is about the same as in the United States and much less than Japan. The predominance of the CAP in the Community budget is justified by the fact that it is the only truly integrated sector, and as such is vital to the Community's existence. Net agricultural exporters say that those who consider that the budget is inequitable should remember all the benefits conferred by the Community which are not reflected in the budget, for example, free trade in industrial products. (They seem to discount the non-budget benefits to them generated by the CAP.) To reduce spending on the CAP is a backward step that could prove fatal to the Community as a whole. It is argued, therefore, that the Community's own resources should instead be increased by raising the ceiling on their VAT element.

Some governments are firmly opposed to expanding own resources. Moreover, this would require the approval of national parliaments, which in general are less sympathetic than governments to the idea. Part of the explanation is that in the current climate of recession national public finances are meeting with difficulty. Some member states insist that before agreeing to an increase in revenue they want restructuring to achieve more balanced expenditure among the various policies, and hence among member states. Others would like first to see the discipline of the own resources ceiling effect a tightening up of the operation of the CAP that would leave it more efficient and less open to criticism. For the time being, raising the VAT ceiling is not a practical proposal, though it will be kept on the agenda.

Proposals

The inclusion in the UK budget agreement of 30 May 1980 of a request to the Commission to examine the development of Community policies and draw up proposals for restructuring the budget opened up the prospect of reforming the CAP. Referring to it in a statement to the House of Lords on 2 June, the foreign secretary, Lord Carrington, said: 'This together with the restraints imposed by the one per cent ceiling, will enable us to press for lasting reforms, which will, among other things, resolve the British budgetary problem.' The hope that restructuring would induce changes in the CAP that would lead to its eventual reform was not universally shared. The farm sector, some of the member governments and DG VI were, on the contrary, intent on ensuring that restructuring was effected in a way that would leave the CAP essentially unchanged.

During the following months numerous suggestions were put forward for coping with the budgetary cost of the CAP. There were two main lines of approach: either to lower the cost or to shift it away from the Community budget. Since by far the largest part of expenditure on the CAP was for price support, this meant either curbing excess production or finding alternative means of paying for it. Many proposals combined the two approaches and contained several elements.

Although proposals for lowering the cost of the CAP generally focused on curbing excess production, they included ways of making savings on the way the CAP operates: for example, more selective management of the intervention system; more rigorous application of quality controls; the reduction or removal of some special subsidies and premiums; and a more astute export policy. This last would comprise lowering the level of export restitutions by timing exports more carefully and by collaborating with other exporting countries in organizing world markets so as to keep world prices closer to Community prices. Other possibilities were long-term supply contracts, notably with Middle East countries, and an expanded food-aid policy, perhaps using substantial buffer stocks and commercially financed export credit. Such savings would not alone reduce costs adequately. Some of them − for example, quality control or the disappearance of particular subsidies and premiums − would entail costs to some member states and not to others.

To curb excess production, either quantitative restrictions or a restrictive price policy are proposed. Quantitative restrictions imply some form of quota system, whereby each farmer is allotted a specific amount of production that can be sold at the support price. This reduces the cost of price support and discourages farmers from producing above their quota. Quotas already exist for sugar: full price support is provided up to a basic level, reduced price support up to a second level and no price support above that. The quotas are determined for the Community as a whole and then distributed among producers according to their size.

Quotas could have a more direct impact on surpluses than would other measures, but they are difficult to negotiate and administer, and have some adverse effects. The negotiating problems arise in the distribution of quotas among countries and among farms. It is easier to reach agreement if quotas are set at a high level. There is then downward rigidity: that is, when market circumstances indicate that quotas should be raised, they will be; but when the indications are that they should be lowered, they will not. Administration is complicated, in varying degrees according to the country and the product, by the need to collect large amounts of information and to maintain extensive control over marketing. For sugar this does not present difficulties because all production has to be processed in a refinery before it can be sold; the marketing of cereals is highly organized in France and the UK, but less so in Germany; dairy products are distributed through numerous small outlets in some countries. A variant that avoids some of the disadvantages of quotas is differential prices, whereby the full price is paid on a basic amount and lower prices on subsequent amounts. Since the amounts are the same for all farms, small farmers can sell their entire production at the full price, while larger farmers sell part of their production at lower prices.

Unless there is provision for transferring them, quotas freeze the existing structure of production, reduce competitiveness and impede increases in productivity. There is too a risk of production from net exporters being dumped on net importers and of trade barriers being set up in retaliation. In so far as quantitative restrictions curb budget costs, they may reduce pressure for price restraint. If excessively high prices do result, it may become impossible to remove quotas because the price reduction that would then be needed to avoid a massive increase in production would be politically unacceptable. Thus quotas, though intended as a short-term measure, might become permanent.

A measure that comes somewhere between quantitative restrictions and a restrictive price policy is a quantum scheme. The term quantum causes some confusion because it originated in France, where it referred to quotas with differential prices, but it is now more generally used to describe something like the UK's former standard-quantity system for cereals. In this sense a quantum entails setting a level of production for the whole Community and lowering intervention prices in proportion to the amount by which production exceeds the level that was set. A quantum scheme would have a direct effect on prices and would avoid most of the negotiating and administrative difficulties associated with quotas, though setting the total level of production might still present problems. It would not, however, provide scope for discriminating between large and small producers, and it would mean that farmers would not know what price they were to receive until after their crops had been harvested.

A restrictive price policy could be implemented by agreement at the annual price-fixing, either to freeze prices or sharply to curtail increases. This would be technically straightforward but politically difficult, particularly since it would require taking a long view. Response of supply and demand to changes in agricultural prices is often slow. Indeed, on the supply side there may be initially a perverse reaction to lower prices as producers increase their production in an effort to maintain their income level. Furthermore, since productivity is rising, a small price reduction no more than offsets that effect and does not bring about a decline in the amount produced. To have the desired impact on surpluses, price cuts need to be comparatively large and sustained.

Any reduction in the prices received by farmers will, given continuing increases in costs, be a squeeze on their income. The poorest farmers, particularly those in countries with high inflation rates, would suffer severe hardship. Since maintaining farm income is the overriding objective of the CAP, proposals for a restrictive price policy are often coupled with schemes for income support or structural policy. As a Community policy, direct aid to incomes would be costly, and determining the level at which income should be maintained would be a problem in view of the divergence among member states. It would do nothing to encourage poor farmers either to go out of production or to adapt their farms. Direct income support might be more appropriately organized at national level, but this line encounters the difficulty that poor farmers predominate in poor countries so that the countries that would need to provide most support would be those least able to finance it. The Community's experience of structural policy is not encouraging. It is difficult to implement, slow to take effect and expensive. Modernization may increase production of goods that are already in surplus, while farmers leaving the land may add to an already serious unemployment problem and contribute to rural depopulation, which most member states would like to avoid.

Whereas quantitative restrictions and restrictive price policy are aimed at lowering budgetary costs by reducing excess production, another approach is to find alternative means of financing. Three main

73

possibilities have been canvassed: producer co-responsibility, national financing, and duties and taxes on imported cereal substitutes and vegetable protein. The idea of co-responsibility is that the Community should obtain from producers some financial contribution to the cost of disposing of surpluses. A co-responsibility levy has existed for sugar since 1971, and for milk since 1977. In June 1980 a general levy equal to 2 per cent of the target price was applied to milk producers, except for some in less-favoured areas. The levy is deducted from the price paid to producers and used to finance expenditure on promoting consumption of dairy products. Although the levy is paid by producers, they have received a commensurate increase in support prices, so that it is in fact a tax on consumers. It is a cumbersome financial device that has no impact on excess production, since it neither discourages production nor encourages consumption.

At the 1980 price review, when this levy was agreed, the Agriculture Council decided that if production in the calendar year 1980 rose by more than 1.5 per cent over 1979, a super-levy would be introduced in 1981-2. This super-levy would be more akin to a quantitative restriction, since it entails imposing a higher levy on increases in production. Discussions about its application have raised such problems as what should be taken as the base for determining whether production has increased, and what, if any, exemptions should be allowed. It also seems likely that any percentage that would be acceptable to producers would be too small to bring about a lowering of production.

National financing is proposed for price support that would otherwise require expenditure exceeding the own-resources limit. Either common prices would be partly nationally financed, or common prices would be agreed within the own-resources limit, and member states could provide supplementary support on a national basis. This would violate one of the three principles, but is defended on the grounds that there is ample evidence that member states are able, are willing and need to maintain disparate support policies. In addition, it would curb transfers from net importing to net exporting countries, and would impose some financial restraint on agriculture ministers. Against this it is argued that in principle it would be a retrograde step for the Community, and that in practice member states differ widely in their ability to finance agricultural policy. To increase national financing would add to existing distortions and prompt some member states to erect protective barriers.

Although there have been proposals for imposing or increasing duties on imported cereal substitutes or vegetable protein, this is probably not feasible because of GATT regulations (*see above, p. 47*). An internal tax which applied equally to home-produced and imported vegetable oils and fats would get round the obstacle of GATT. The case for such a tax is that it would not only generate increased revenue but also reduce surpluses: of cereals, because vegetable protein would be more costly, so the demand for cereals would rise, and of dairy products, because the higher cost of inputs would deter some dairy production. The increased cost of soya would encourage pig producers to switch to using skimmed milk for feed; and the higher cost of edible oils would raise the price of margarine and so increase demand for butter. Spain, once it joined the Community, would be greatly affected by this tax, and the Commission has said that the matter should be considered further during the period preceding accession. It is likely that a means would be found of compensating Community producers for the tax, so the cost would fall chiefly on third-country exporters and Community consumers.

While all these measures are aimed at relieving the budgetary costs of the CAP, their non-budget effects would vary widely. The proposals would have contrasting impacts on the allocation of resources; the distribution of income within agriculture and between agriculture and the rest of the economy; non-budget transfers between member states; and trade with third countries. A restrictive price policy accompanied by direct income aids, for example, should in the longer run improve allocation, redistribute income from producers to consumers and from taxpayers to low-income producers, reduce the non-budget transfers from net importing to net exporting countries, and lower the level of protection on trade with third countries. Quantitative restrictions would probably do none of these, and might have opposite effects in some cases. Hence the restructuring of the budget could advance or impede reform.

Attitudes of member states[6]

The attitudes of member states to proposals for changing the CAP in the context of budget restructuring are determined by both political and economic factors. The political weight of farmers in most member states is disproportionate to their numbers and to the importance of agriculture in the economy. In the past, agriculture was a dominant sector of the economy and this was reflected in a country's politics and institutions. Agriculture's position in the economy has undergone a relative decline, but the political habits and the institutions established in its heyday are changing at a much slower pace. In some countries agriculture is almost a state within a state, with a separate political and economic organization. In France, for example, the large agricultural organizations have an elaborate political structure through which farmers channel their political pressure. In Germany, agriculture is protected in a way that runs counter to the free-trade principles that Germany otherwise actively promotes. In most member states, agriculture is the only industry for which there is a separate ministry.

Farming was one of the first industries to build up national organizations and systematically to use political pressure to defend its interests. Other groups have been much less effective. Except in the UK, consumers are a weak pressure group and tend to concentrate on aspects such as quality and the use of additives rather than more political issues such as price levels. The implications for manufacturing industry of changes in the CAP differ among the various branches. To the extent that the CAP encourages farmers to increase production by applying more technically or scientifically advanced methods, it may benefit producers of agricultural machinery or chemicals. For the food-processing industry the CAP entails high raw-material costs, while for industry as a whole high food prices affect wage costs.

Although all these features are generally applicable, the political weight of agriculture differs among member states. There are several reasons for this: the size of the agricultural population varies; in some countries it is concentrated in particular regions, while in others it is more evenly distributed; and the structure of agriculture, particularly farm size and the mix of products, differs.

There is broad agreement among member states that the maintenance of farm income should continue to be the first priority of the CAP. Differences arise as to whether the budgetary and other costs of pursuing this objective should be curbed, and if so how. The attitudes of member states are affected by their net budgetary position, trade flows, and the structure and technical efficiency of their farm sectors.

The smaller member states are generally more convinced than the larger ones of the case for expanding own resources. This is partly because they obtain proportionately large net benefits from the budget, but also because the wider benefits of membership are of greater importance to them. In Denmark, however, there is divergence between the government, which advocates raising the VAT ceiling, and the parliament, which in present economic circumstances would probably vote against it. There is support in Italy for an increase that would provide more resources for Mediterranean regions, though the government has yet to take a definite position. The new government in France seems to be implying that it would, unlike its predecessor, favour an increase, but that it recognizes that this cannot be envisaged at present. Germany and the UK are the only member governments firmly opposed to raising the ceiling.

Net exporting countries resist proposals for restrictions on prices or quantities and suggest dealing with surpluses by expanding exports to third countries. Some, notably Denmark and the Netherlands, would welcome a rationalization of the CAP that made its operation less costly. If they were to agree to a measure of restraint, exporting countries would probably prefer some form of quantum, since they see a high price level as affording advantage to their balances of payments, both through the budget and through trade flows. Importing countries, particularly Germany and the UK, are inclined to favour price restraint.

Proposals that would penalize more efficient farmers result in a different alignment: in livestock rearing, Denmark, the Netherlands and the UK confront the other member states. France, Ireland and Italy have all claimed that at least some of their dairy producers should be granted exemptions from a co-responsibility super-levy. Countries with comparatively efficient agricultural sectors, and also Germany, would accept allowing freer play to market forces within the CAP. Other member states, with a large number of small farmers on low incomes, notably France and Italy, will probably opt for quotas with differential prices or some other arrangement that would mean large farmers receiving guaranteed prices for a smaller proportion of their production than small farmers.

Two institutions that have been involved in consultations at the Community level are the European Parliament and COPA. The Parliament in June 1981, after a lively debate, adopted a resolution from its Agriculture Committee which proposed that there should be a global Community quantum, based on a production target, for each of the products supported by intervention prices. For amounts of production above the quantum the guaranteed price should be progressively lowered. There were signs that COPA too was begining to lean towards a quantum as a solution to the budgetary problems of the CAP, though previously it had considered producer co-responsibility the 'least unacceptable' of the various proposals. In either case it would insist on certain conditions, including the extension of price guarantees to all products, the setting up of instruments for an export policy, and an increase in own resources.

The Commission took account of many of these attitudes in drawing up its proposals for restructuring the budget. Those proposals relating specifically to the CAP were prepared by the Commissioner responsible for agriculture and DG VI, though the Commission as a whole approved them. The evolution of the Commission's views and its report on the restructuring mandate will be considered in the next chapter.

8 The report on the mandate

The mandate given to the Commission, as part of the UK budget agreement, to report on the restructuring of the budget, set in motion the process of lobbying and consultation that accompanies the preparation of major policy decisions on the CAP. Within member states various interested parties, at different levels, fed their views into government decision-making channels. There were some bilateral discussions between member states, and ideas were discussed at Community level in the European Parliament and in COPA. The focus of this activity was the Commission. Private meetings took place between officials from the Commission and officials from member states. In the first instance, it is the Commission which decides what will or will not be included in a proposal and how different points are emphasized, though the Council of Ministers may revise a proposal substantially before it is approved. If a member state can convince the Commission to include its ideas in the proposal that goes to the Council of Ministers, it will start out with an advantage when the Council comes to consider the proposal.

In December 1980 the Commission published a document in which it presented its 'orientations' for the overhaul of the CAP which now had to be undertaken. *Reflections on the CAP* was to contribute to the Commission's examination of all the common policies and their budgetary aspects. Although it was not formally discussed by the Council of Ministers or at official level, the paper received widespread attention and was the subject of informal exchanges of views. The 1981 price review, which began in February, was expected to indicate how seriously member governments were responding to the ideas being circulated for revising the CAP and reducing its budgetary cost. Agreement on the price review was reached at the start of April, and later that month the Commission began in earnest to draft its report on the 30 May mandate.

Reflections on the CAP

As its title indicates, this is a reflective document. There are three main sections: the first considers the purpose of the CAP and its results so far; the second analyses the difficulties that it has encountered; and the third puts forward solutions. The first section sets out the original reasons for establishing free trade in agricultural products. It reaffirms the essential role of the three principles and goes to some lengths to justify them and to stress their indivisibility. The CAP could not be based on a system that was radically different from price support, though special problems could be solved by Community measures for direct income support. The document suggests that the five objectives are being satisfactorily fulfilled.

Four areas of criticism are identified. The first is that the price support afforded by the CAP results in a continual increase in production and consequently an uncontrollable rise in expenditure. The second and third criticisms are that the CAP works to the advantage of larger producers and of richer regions. These three criticisms are implicitly accepted.

Budgetary aspects of the CAP make up the fourth criticism. Two points are directly rebutted: the CAP should not be blamed either for the absolute size of agricultural expenditure or for its share in the budget. The document acknowledges that the CAP results in unequal budget transfers among member states, but suggests that these derive from the very structure of the Community and do not alone 'justify a reconsideration of the single common policy – agriculture'. It is implied that the benefits that some states receive from the CAP are purely budgetary, and need to be set against the economic returns to others from the common market in industrial products. The most pertinent aspect of criticism of the budget is, in the Commission's view, directed against the way in which agricultural funds are spent on ever larger surpluses without reducing income disparities in agriculture. This calls for certain amendments to the CAP, though 'a decrease in agricultural expenditure is unlikely to solve what is generally known as the Community's budget restructuring problem'.

Turning to solutions, the paper lists what should be the aims of adjustments to the CAP: to maintain the CAP's positive achievements; check its budgetary consequences; arrive at a better distribution of benefits among regions; and organize the Community's finances so as not to cause disputes among member states. It rejects a solution that includes national financing: if member states were able to provide additional support on top of common prices, the result would be a 'price cocktail'; if prices were commonly agreed but partly financed by member states, the result would also be an end to common prices since, if the cost fell on their own budgets, some member states would not agree to the high prices desired by others.[1] Also discarded is any scheme simply for redistributing financial burdens among member states.

Solutions, the Commission says, must be sought along three lines: adjustment of market organizations; a new approach to export policy; and adaptation of structural policy. With regard to market organization, the most important element is co-responsibility or producer participation. This should become the fourth basic principle of the CAP: 'Any production above a certain volume, to be fixed taking into account the internal consumption of the Community and its external trade, must be charged fully or partially to the producers.' The application of co-responsibility would vary among products. It could take the form of a levy, a price reduction or a quantum, but not quotas. Nor should the idea of national co-responsibility levies, on those member states where production is increasing, be pursued. There should also be changes in the way the intervention system is managed. In the context of external trade, the Commission intends to curb imports of cereal substitutes and protein supplements, and to seek long-term export contracts. Lastly, the increasing use of structural measures as an instrument of social policy should continue.

The document is disjointed, and hence inconsistent. It rehearses the familiar justifications of the CAP but also concurs with some uncompromising criticisms. The paper is ambivalent about the basic problem of restructuring, objecting to a financial solution but also arguing that reduced agricultural expenditure will not solve the problem. The central argument seems to be that it is either not possible or not desirable to reduce further the number of farmers or to maintain farm income other than by the present policy of price support, but since this policy results in excess production and so in large expenditure, some form of tax should be imposed on farmers. Apparently this is intended to fall more heavily on larger farmers, both on distributional grounds and because they are chiefly responsible for increased production. The prescriptions, however, are vague (perhaps deliberately so) and in some respects do not correspond to the diagnosis.

The document leaned towards the views of the then French government, though it attempted to provide something to please most people. In the event it displeased most people. The proposed extension of co-responsibility was not well received. Farmers saw it as at best the least of the various evils being suggested as ways of reducing the cost of the CAP. The vagueness of the proposals made their likely impact difficult to evaluate, but there was doubt as to whether they would adequately curb expenditure on the CAP. It was pointed out that clawing back money from farmers was a less effective way of cutting costs than lowering prices. Member states with efficient agriculture sectors suspected that co-responsibility measures would penalize them.

The 1981 price review

The Commission presented its proposals for the 1981 price review in February. They included price increases ranging from 6 per cent to 12 per cent and averaging 7.8 per cent; the elimination of MCAs for Belgium, Luxembourg and the Netherlands, and a reduction of 5 per cent in the MCAs of Germany and the UK; a co-responsibility super-levy on milk of up to 30 per cent for certain levels of output; and a more general suggestion for extending co-responsibility to other products. The proposals were greeted with outrage on all sides. Agricultural organizations condemned the price increases for being too small; COPA, which had called for a 15.3 per cent increase, described the proposals as 'a gross provocation'. Responses from member governments were less forthright but most of them indicated dissatisfaction. Within the Commission those responsible for the budget criticized the proposed price increases as too high. They were much higher than in the previous three years when the Commission's pursuit of a 'prudent' price policy had led to a fall in real producer prices.

The Council of Ministers discussed the proposals at the end of

February and again a month later. Eight delegations insisted on larger price increases than the Commission was proposing. France, backed by Ireland and others, rejected the broadening of co-responsibility, arguing that this was too reformist and should be debated in the context of restructuring. Only the UK supported the proposals on prices and co-responsibility, while Germany acquiesced on the price increases. Both, however, were unwilling to revalue their green rates.

Yet another prolonged and agonizing series of negotiations seemed to be in prospect. Every member government was at odds with at least one of the essential points of the proposals. Thanks to the rise in world prices during the previous year, the prospect of the budget resources being exhausted had receded.[2] Governments were more inclined to respond to pressure from their farm sectors. France, however, with a presidential election imminent, was anxious to achieve a quick settlement, and had obtained an undertaking, written into the UK budget agreement, that member states would 'do their best to ensure that Community decisions are taken expeditiously', particularly those on the 1981 price review. This undertaking had been reaffirmed at the EEC heads of government Summit in Maastricht just before the Agriculture Council met.

Two events hastened a decision. On 21 March the Italian lira had been devalued by 6 per cent. Subsequently there was a 23 per cent revaluation of sterling against its theoretical ECU rate, largely reflecting the rise in sterling over the past year. This, described officially in the UK as a purely technical move triggered by the Italian devaluation and by the Dutch agriculture minister as 'a gift from heaven', raised the ECU's rate against other EMS currencies by 2.5 per cent and set in motion a realignment of market rates. It was agreed that France, Italy, Denmark, Ireland and Greece would devalue their green rates by amounts ranging from 2.5 per cent to 8 per cent. Any price rises that were agreed would in effect be increased by the amount of the green-rate devaluations of these countries, which were the ones pushing hardest for higher prices.

On 26 March, after extensive amendments, the European Parliament approved a report of its Agriculture Committee calling for an average 12 per cent price increase and rejecting most of the Commission's proposals for controlling excess production and costs.[3] The Commission retreated on its price proposals and presented to the Council on 1 April a revised package involving average increases of 9.45 per cent. It continued trying to defend its plans to extend co-responsibility. The UK held out against the price increase until it had obtained agreement that its green rate should not be revalued, and that the consumer subsidy for butter and the premium for beef farmers would be retained.

To the traditional accompaniment of farmers throwing eggs and firecrackers, and Belgian riot police discharging tear gas, agreement on the revised price increases was reached on 2 April. The Commission largely failed in its efforts to push co-responsibility. It was decided to raise the general dairy levy from 2 per cent to 2.5 per cent, and to bring in a super-levy if support costs should escalate by more than 1 per cent as a result of increased supplies in 1981 as against 1980. There was some bewilderment, particularly in France, at the role that the UK had played in facilitating agreement. The UK government denied that it had acted to assist M. Giscard d'Estaing in his election campaign. Perhaps more relevant was the fact that under the UK's budget agreement it would be able to recoup part of the additional costs that it would incur as a result of the price increases. The outcome of the price review indicated to the Commission that while member governments, or at least their agriculture ministers, might eventually mend their ways on price rises and co-responsibility, like St Augustine they hoped it would not happen yet. Against this background the Commission set out to prepare its report on the restructuring mandate.

The report on the mandate

The Commission presented its report in the last week of June. Like the *Reflections on the CAP*, it is in places vague or ambiguous and occasionally self-contradictory. The cause seems to have been that the final draft was prepared in haste, with several last-minute revisions, and translated from the original French in even greater haste. Perhaps also some differences within the Commission remained unresolved when the final text of the document was drawn up. The effect is that the reader has difficulty discerning what, if any, meaning to read into some passages and reconciling what is said in one place with what is said in another. Although negotiations may be facilitated if proposals of this sort are not set out in too much detail, they may be hampered if the imprecision is such that even the broad intent is obscured.

The Commission endeavours to set the mandate within a wide framework. The opening paragraphs of its report speak of the duty to defend and develop the shared inheritance that already exists by devising a joint strategy for tackling the economic problems besetting the Community. In the fifth paragraph the Commission calls for a return to institutional balance, which presumably includes reinforcing the role of the Commission, and says that it will take the necessary steps to overcome the constraint imposed on Community activities by the current ceiling on budget resources.

The report then commends the evolution of the single internal market for industrial goods and the common agricultural policy but acknowledges that other policies have not advanced at the same pace and that changes in the international economy have generated new requirements. There follows a convoluted paragraph, which begins by stating that the budget reflects the imbalance among policies, but then says that the budget does not give the full picture, because some policies have no budgetary dimension while others have so far affected the budget too little to signify. Moreover, Community policies 'have economic implications far transcending the budget aspect', which 'is why the Commission has chosen not to confine itself to a purely budgetary view in implementing its mandate'. The next eight paragraphs deal with the areas in which the Community needs to progress. Closer coordination is needed of member states' monetary and economic policies, which would be greatly facilitated by expansion of the European Monetary System. The customs union should be completed by eliminating the various trade barriers that still remain. A new strategy is required for energy and for advanced technology, and an active competition policy is essential.

After setting out this list, however, the report avers in paragraph 17 that 'it is hard to see how the Community can hope to advance in a balanced, decisive fashion on these various points unless it puts its budgetary affairs in order'. The Commission's proposals, it continues, concern essentially the common agricultural policy, regional policy and social policy, and paragraph 18 specifies that 'The major effort concerns the common agricultural policy'. The CAP is thus placed firmly in the context of budgetary problems. Despite the earlier assertion that Community policies have economic implications far transcending the budget, scant attention is paid to the non-budget effects of the CAP. The Commission does state that it is neither economically sensible nor financially possible fully to guarantee prices for products in structural surplus and, in an awkward and oracular phrase, that 'bearing consumers' interests in mind, prices must reflect market realities more than they have in the past'. Nonetheless, all references to costs relate only to budget costs. The guidelines on which future decisions should be based 'should be combined to achieve the objectives set by the Treaty at as low a cost as possible'. That the object of the guidelines is budgetary is reiterated in paragraph 31, at the end of the section on the CAP: if applied, they 'will mean that agricultural spending in the years ahead will grow less rapidly than the Community's own resources'.

The following eight paragraphs are concerned with regional and social policy. The report notes that the Regional and Social Funds are due to be revised by the end of 1981 and in 1982 respectively. A framework for these revisions is set out, and some suggestions are made about the future operation of the borrowing and lending operations. Policy needs to be better coordinated and more efficiently administered. Regional policy should concentrate more on the most deprived areas, while social policy should give priority to job creation. In the Commission's view, if the two Funds are to attain their objectives, appropriations to them will have to grow faster than the total budget.

At this point the report restates the intention of the Commission to propose that own resources be increased 'when this becomes necessary to achieve agreed objectives'. It then acknowledges that the Commission's recommendations could not have a significant impact on the budget for some time. In five of the six main categories of budget expenditure this creates no particular problem, but the pattern of appropriations from the Guarantee Section of FEOGA results under present circumstances in an inequitable situation for the United Kingdom. To correct this imbalance the UK could receive compensation, which would be assessed by comparing its share of the Community's GNP with the proportion it obtains of guarantee expenditure. This compensation, which would continue long enough for the effects of the new guidelines to be felt, would be financed from the budget or, if budget expenditure continues to rise and the own-resources ceiling is not raised, possibly by abatements on other member states' receipts from the Community.

In the final three paragraphs the report returns to the wider context of the Commission's deliberations. Noting that it has scarcely touched on many areas of Community activity, such as external relations, the report suggests, however, that the priority measures proposed would provide a major impetus to 'relaunching the whole development of the Community', which in turn would strengthen its position on the international economic stage. The Commission has outlined the way forward: the other institutions should now take the necessary political decision.

The broad appeal with which the report closes is in contrast with its earlier treatment of agricultural policy. Not only is the CAP dealt with solely in a budgetary context, but even within the confines of the budget no major shift is envisaged. The Commission sets its guidelines for the CAP with the modest aim of ensuring that spending on it grows less rapidly than the own resources. For some years the proportion of the budget devoted to the CAP will remain large, and a special mechanism involving sizable refunds will be needed if the United Kingdom's inordinate contribution to the budget is to be reduced.

New guidelines for the CAP

The section dealing with the new guidelines for the CAP begins by commending the CAP for achieving, on balance, a positive result over the past twenty years. It has fulfilled the objectives of the Treaty of Rome: security of food supplies, satisfaction of consumer's requirements, increased productivity and higher farm incomes. This has been done for a total cost which, at 0.5 per cent of GDP, is not excessive when compared either with what it would cost each member to run its own national policy or with the cost of the policies of the Community's main competitors.

Recalling the instruction in the mandate that the basic principles of the CAP should not be called into question, the report confirms that these remain essential. Nor is it possible or desirable to jettison the mechanisms of the CAP, though to adjust them is both possible and necessary. The report indicates that the necessity arises from the existence of surpluses in most major products. Surpluses are the unwelcome effects of technological progress and 'the operation of market organizations'. 'The imperatives of sound market management' and budgetary constraints require that there should be 'improved control' of surpluses. The Commission has concluded that guaranteed prices should not be fixed with respect solely to farm income considerations but should reflect market realities more than they have, and that the guarantee should no longer be open-ended.

Having established this frame of reference, the Commission sets out its seven guidelines for future decisions on the CAP.

(1) Price policy and (2) export policy are highly interdependent in the context of the Commission's recommendation that the Community should aim gradually to align guaranteed prices with prices ruling 'on a better organized world market'. This could be achieved by pursuing a rigorous policy towards prices within the Community and adopting a more active export policy designed to stabilize world prices by means of cooperation agreements with other major exporters, possibly supplemented by long-term export contracts. What the Commission appears to have in mind is in the short run to continue the existing policy of trying to keep Community price increases to modest proportions, and in the long run to collaborate with other major suppliers to raise the level of world prices. If it can be arranged that over a period of years world prices rise faster than Community prices, the gap between them can be narrowed. This suggests that the need to make prices reflect market realities would in part be met by making realities adjust to prices.

(3) Production targets are proposed to make producers more aware of market realities. They should be set for all major products to signify the volume of production that the Community wants to guarantee at the full price. The Commission has indicated that the target level might equate to more or less than self-sufficiency, depending on the product. It has yet to specify the criteria that should be applied, but for each product they would take into account trends in production and consumption, the degree of self-sufficiency desired, import commitments, export markets and food-aid requirements. Once the target was reached, producers would no longer receive the full price. Again, the arrangements would vary among products: for sugar, the existing quota system should continue; for cereals, tonnages above the production target should receive a lower intervention price; for dairy products, co-responsibility should be extended, or else, the Commission warns, other measures will be inevitable.

(4) Structural policy should be tailored to the needs of individual agricultural regions. Measures are to be prepared to assist in resolving the problems of Mediterranean agriculture, and will be presented to the Council and Parliament before the end of 1982. These will be medium-term programmes covering an integrated policy for incomes, markets, production and structures, and involving both financial and agricultural instruments of the Community.

(5) Income support subsidies are envisaged as a possible supplementary measure in specific circumstances. Since the criteria for granting them would be established by the Community, they might be partly financed by the Community; in view of the cost involved, they would have to be confined to certain small producers.

(6) Quality control and financial control should be reinforced. More rigorous quality control would help reduce surpluses by excluding some production from the scope of the market organizations and would also contribute to export promotion. Tighter financial control would mean the Commission regulating the way that Community financing of intervention is managed in the member states.

(7) National aids are to be subjected to greater discipline by the Commission.

The Commission has indicated that the two guidelines to which it attaches greatest importance are price policy and production targets. It is evident, however, that what the Commission intends by price policy is not immediate price reductions accompanied by generalized income support. Care has been taken to emphasize that income support is proposed only on a highly selective basis. Hence a price policy that is sufficiently restrictive to reduce surpluses is implicitly rejected; instead price policy will be directed towards reducing the budgetary cost of surpluses. Additional pressure on farmers to curb production will be exerted through production targets. The trend towards gearing structural policy to reducing regional imbalance is reinforced. The Commission also signals its intention to reassert control over the CAP by streamlining its operation and curtailing national aid. An unstated corollary was that national financing of price support would not be countenanced. The implications of the Commission's proposals and the prospects for negotiations are considered in the final chapter.

9 Prospects for reforming the CAP

The Commission's proposals

The guidelines in the Commission's report on the mandate are not a proposal for reforming the CAP. Their object is to reduce the budgetary cost of excess production. This is to be achieved in two ways: price policy and export policy are to ensure that the cost of supporting each unit of production is reduced; and production targets are to ensure that the amount of production that receives support is reduced. How feasible such an approach might be is not clear.

Almost half the expenditure under the Guarantee Section is for export restitutions, which are determined by the difference between Community prices and world prices. If this gap could be reduced, export restitutions would cost less. Moreover, if the Community could export a larger proportion of its excess production it could further reduce costs, since it is cheaper to dispose of production by exporting it than by holding it in intervention stocks. The Commission proposes that the Community should pursue a rigorous price policy and a more active export policy, including collaboration with other major suppliers to boost world prices.

For the past few years the Commission has tried to pursue a prudent price policy. It first stated in 1977 that farm income considerations should not be the sole factor determining prices, and, in the following three price reviews, increases were kept to modest amounts. Because maintaining farm income has continued to be the overriding objective, the prudent price policy has encountered a problem common to incomes policies: a squeeze on income can be sustained for only a limited period before pressure builds up to restore relative positions. In 1981 vociferous complaints from farmers, accentuated by the imminence of the French presidential election, induced the Council of Ministers to agree to a price rise of almost 9.5 per cent. The 1982 price review will indicate how earnestly member states have taken the Commission's proposals, but even if on that occasion prices are not increased by much, past performance suggests that it may prove difficult to continue this restraint.

Hope that world prices can be eased upwards has been encouraged by recent success with dairy products. During 1980 extensive informal cooperation between the Community and New Zealand helped push up world prices. To prevent this trend being drastically reversed, the New Zealand Dairy Board agreed in August 1981, 'in self defence' in the words of its chairman, to buy from the United States 100,000 tons of butter at a cost of £85m.

Cooperation with major suppliers in managing world prices may turn out to be problematic in other products as well as dairy. As the OPEC countries have found, for a cartel to succeed in constantly pushing up prices requires either demand to rise or supply to fall. Some advocates of this approach appear to assume that world demand for agricultural products is on a steadily rising trend. This is a debatable point, on which forecasters are divided. Many developing countries are desperately short of food, but except in the case of cereals the Community's excess production does not match their needs. More important, these countries may be unable to pay for the amounts of food that they need so that their demand will not be felt in the market. If demand does not rise, the feasibility of the first leg of the Commission's proposal will depend on whether supply can be curbed.

Curbing supply is the object of the second leg, production targets. Setting these at an appropriate level will be difficult, as the Commission is aware. Although the report asserts that 'For sugar, an effective system is already in operation', the Community's experience with sugar quotas demonstrates that quantitative restrictions present similar pitfalls to those of a price policy: it will be easier to reach agreement if the quantity is set at a high level; and there will downward rigidity. If the target is set at a reasonable level, the pressures on prices will be stronger, both because the squeeze on farm income will be greater, and because it will be argued that to the extent that the quantity is smaller there is scope for a higher price.

Problems will also arise over whether there should be only a Community target or whether this should then be distributed among countries. For example, the Commission proposed that for cereals the target should correspond roughly to domestic consumption. The intervention price for production above the target would be reduced in proportion to the amount of the excess: if the target was exceeded by 3 per cent, the price would be lowered by 3 per cent. This would mean that if production was above the target, all producers would receive a lower price, even though in one country production might have fallen. Similarly, if one country used national aids to boost production above the target, all countries would receive lower prices. On the other hand, to distribute the quantum among member states would entail difficult negotiations.

In preparing its guidelines, the Commission has evidently taken note of some of the reactions it received to its *Reflections on the CAP*. Co-responsibility has been relegated to a smaller role and replaced by production targets. Whereas French concern about imported cereal substitutes and vegetable protein was emphasized in *Reflections*, the report on the mandate seeks to cater for the interests of all the exporting countries with its proposals for aligning Community and world prices, an idea that was strongly promoted by the Danish government. It is questionable whether these policies would have the desired effect on the cost of excess production, however, even assuming that they were approved by the member governments. Nonetheless, there is much to be said for a policy mechanism such as production targets which involves taking a medium-term view of agriculture in the Community as a whole, and it would also be politic for the Community to adopt a more cooperative approach to the world market.

The Commission's proposals would leave the principles and mechanisms of the CAP essentially intact while adjusting the mechanisms to cause budget expenditure to rise less rapidly than the own resources. At least for the next few years, the main burden of restructuring the budget would be left to a budget mechanism. The Commission rejected Germany's contention that it, like the UK, was in an 'unacceptable situation', saying that the German situation was unaccepted rather than unacceptable. No figures were presented to indicate the amount of compensation that the UK would receive or the impact on other member states' net budgetary position. It has been reported that a confidential Commission memorandum calculates that the most the UK could obtain in 1982 would be ECU 1.5 bn. If this were financed by abatements on other member states' receipts, the effects would be as shown in the table.

Forecast gains (+) and losses (−) from EEC budget in 1982 (£m)

	No change in rules	Change proposed by Commission*
UK	−1578	−691
Germany	−851	−1071
Greece	+65	+54
France	+165	−53
Luxembourg	+189	+188
Netherlands	+284	+151
Denmark	+325	+258
Belgium	+361	+291
Ireland	+431	+382
Italy	+609	+492

* Assuming a refund to Britain ECU 1.5bn (£887m).
Source: *The Economist*, 19 September 1981.

Member states' reactions

The Commission presented its report to the Community's heads of government at the European Council meeting in Luxembourg on 29 and 30 June 1981. It was agreed in advance that, in view of the recent change of government in France, the Council would note but not discuss the report. Both the British prime minister and the German chancellor, Helmut Schmidt, at the end of the summit, criticized the Commission for confining its proposals for making the budget more equitable to a specific arrangement for the UK, rather than providing for an equitable distribution of the burden of financing Europe.

Helmut Schmidt stressed that Germany's payments were running at about 20 per cent of the estimated DM 30 bn. deficit on its balance-of-payments current account. There was 'no reason why other equally rich countries should not pay a proportionally similar amount' to the Community budget as Germany. This was a reference to Denmark in particular, but also to Belgium, the Netherlands and Luxembourg. None of these countries is enthusiastic about the idea of a more general corrective mechanism, though as small countries they would all welcome steps to strengthen the Community. The Dutch foreign minister has said that the share of the CAP in budget expenditure should be reduced from 70 per cent to 60 per cent by the beginning of 1984.

The Commission's report contains proposals that would benefit the three least prosperous member states: Greece and Italy would gain from the structural measures for the Mediterranean, and Ireland from increased spending on regional and social policy. It was also suggested that if the compensation to the UK was to be financed through abatements, these should fall less heavily on Ireland, Greece and Italy. These three governments would probably find the budget arrangements acceptable. There was little initial response from the new French government. Virtually all the reactions focused on the specifically budgetary aspects of the proposals. No doubt the proposals for the CAP took longer to digest.

Timing of negotiations

At the Luxembourg summit it was agreed to establish a working group comprising the member states' permanent representatives to the Communities. The group is to try to agree the broad lines of approach to the Commission's proposals for the CAP and the budget. It was set up in an attempt to avoid the proposals for the CAP being negotiated by the Agriculture Council. Although it is an *ad hoc* group, its membership is very similar to that of Coreper. Coreper is reckoned to be very much dominated by national interests, and it is not clear how constructively many of the same individuals meeting as a working group will tackle their task of defining in detail the approaches of member states to the key issues.

The heads of government will discuss the proposal at the next meeting of the European Council in London in November 1981, and the agriculture ministers will certainly have a hand in negotiations when the Commission presents its proposals for the 1982 price review in February. Negotiations on restructuring are likely to be protracted. Some Commission officials believe that they could extend beyond the time when the own resources become exhausted, which at present seems likely to be in 1983.

It seems to be assumed that if this happened member states would make supplementary contributions to the budget, until such time as restructuring had been settled and they were ready to negotiate an increase in own resources. These contributions could be determined in line with the GNP-based contributions that member states used to make before the VAT-based system of own resources was introduced. A transitional arrangement such as this would not come about automatically, however. It would have to be agreed among member states, though it would not need the approval of their parliaments. If negotiations on restructuring were proceeding to its dissatisfaction, or for some other reason, a member government could refuse to agree to supplementary contributions. Were the Community to run short of money, the Guarantee Section of FEOGA would be the last item of expenditure to be affected, because it is classed as obligatory expenditure, whereas most other items are non-obligatory. The day might come, however, when the Community had inadequate finance even to cover Guarantee Section expenditure. There would then be national financing of the CAP *de facto* if not *de jure*.

The possibility of the Community being inadequately financed would also interact with enlargement. A neat scenario put forward in the Commission is that, since both enlargement and an increase in own resources will require the approval of national parliaments, and since enlargement is due at the beginning of 1984 and own resources may run out in 1983, the two issues could be linked and approval for both obtained simultaneously. If approval for an increase in own resources were not forthcoming, the Community would have either to postpone enlargement, which would be politically damaging, or to take in two additional less-prosperous members at a time when it was short of funds.

Clearly the next two or three years will see some very tough negotiating over the budget, in which the CAP will be a central issue. This prospect presents opportunity and risk. The opportunity lies in the possibility that budgetary imperatives could force changes that would make the CAP more rational. The risk is that budget problems will be solved by shifting the costs of the CAP away from the budget, making them more obscure and still more difficult to tackle. Changes in the CAP are in any case likely to be piecemeal. Because they will probably take place in the context of budgetary pressures, it will be particularly necessary to bear in mind what the long-run objectives of CAP reform should be, so as to ensure that short-run tactics tilt developments in a propitious direction.

Long-run objectives

The Commission is right to say that the amount of budget expenditure on the CAP should not be the central issue in discussions about changing the CAP. More significant is how money is spent and how it is distributed, among individuals and among member states. Whether by criteria of economic efficiency, social welfare or equity among member states, the CAP is deficient. It wastefully encourages production for which there is no demand, redistributes income in a way that favours the better-off more than the needy, and causes resources to be transferred between member states in a haphazard and often inequitable manner. The reason for this is that within the CAP prices are expected to perform two functions: to balance supply and demand, and to subsidize farm income. Prices have been too low to provide an adequate income for farmers with high costs, but high enough to signal to low-cost producers to raise output.

The gap between supply and demand is widening steadily, and can be satisfactorily reduced only by lowering prices. If it continues to increase, the CAP will eventually collapse. The CAP was intended to enable the agricultural exporting countries to increase their exports to the rest of the Community. Initially this happened, but the incentives of the system to producers were such that all countries, except Italy, increased their self-sufficiency. This has reduced outlets for exporters within the Community. The share of France, for example, in intra-Community agricultural exports has declined noticeably, and France's balance of agricultural trade with the rest of the Community has deteriorated sharply. In trade with the Community, France's agricultural imports amounted to 43 per cent of its exports in 1973, but this figure rose to 66 per cent in 1979. The government of M. Giscard d'Estaing responded by pressing for the Community to adopt an aggressive export policy. To continue, however, to produce increasing amounts of goods that cannot be sold without subsidy is not a sustainable policy. Sooner or later the subsidy will grow so large that the Community will be unable or unwilling to pay for it.

If in their role of signalling to producers the amount demanded prices need to be lowered, something else will have to take on their role of maintaining farm income. The option that is most often advanced is direct income aids. These have been proposed by both parties in the German coalition government, albeit in a modified version in the case of the SPD. The French Ministry of the Economy has presented plans for price reductions accompanied by income subsidies in the dairy sector. A policy of price restraint, combined with direct income aids, has several attractions: it would enable the objectives of reasonable prices for consumers and a fair standard of living for farmers to be pursued at the same time; it would be in accordance with the CAP's three principles; it could be directed specifically to benefit small farmers; and it would reduce export subsidies, and so improve relations between the Community and the rest of the world in the context of agricultural trade.

Such a thoroughgoing reform is not about to happen, and may never happen, but if the CAP is to make a more positive contribution to the Community, that is the direction in which it should be pointed. The political obstacles in its way should not be underestimated: farmers automatically oppose price reductions, and those not eligible for income support would lose. Moreover, farmers maintain the myth that, under the present system, their prices, and hence their income, are derived entirely from the market. Although a lower price and a direct income subsidy would comprise the same elements as the present price, which comes partly from the market and partly from a subsidy, farmers say that they would find it demeaning to receive an income subsidy. Member governments continue to believe that the farm sector is politically important and so often defer to farmers' views. Perhaps most important, a policy of this sort might require, at least to begin with, an increase in budget expenditure. Its immediate advantage would be its effects on non-budget costs and on distribution. But if producers responded to the new price levels in the first instance by increasing production, the budgetary cost of price support might not be reduced sufficiently to offset the cost of income subsidies. This is probably the reason why the report on the mandate implicity rejects direct income aids.

Short-term tactics

The purpose of negotiations on restructuring will be to lower the budgetary cost of the CAP. The purpose of a reform of the CAP would be to lower the total cost, and to redistribute costs and benefits more equitably. It means lowering prices, but might for a time generate higher budget costs. The implication for the restructuring negotiations is that efforts to shift costs away from the budget, for example, by a co-responsibility levy, without reducing total costs should be resisted. The exception would be national financing, which would probably impose the greatest burdens on the exchequers of those member states that currently push the hardest for price increases.

The UK government should dwell less than at present on the budget costs of the CAP. A better CAP would not necessarily be cheaper in budgetary terms. By overemphasizing budget costs, the UK may impede the path to improving the CAP. The UK should, however, pursue the idea of establishing controls on budget allocations to the CAP. Budget control would not in itself contribute to restructuring, but it would be an indirect means of meeting the German demand for a ceiling on net contributions. Furthermore, if agriculture ministers had to keep within an allocation for farm-price support, they would have to resist more of the political pressure from farm interests. Given their susceptibility, it may be that budget control is a prerequisite for any reform, since without it they would be unable to effect reform proposals.

In a more general context it is necessary to sort out the social from the economic strands of the CAP. Agriculture is a sector in relative decline throughout the Community, and there are strong social arguments for supporting it. There are also economic security arguments, but they are different. The social arguments are that poor farmers should not be obliged to leave the land, particularly at a time when probably the only alternative is unemployment. This is an acceptable case for devoting public money to support the incomes of those who would otherwise suffer hardship. It does not justify devoting even more public money to those who on social grounds have no need of it. At least a quarter (some 2 million) of the Community's farmers are being subsidized unnecessarily, and to a much larger extent than the other three-quarters. This is indefensible at a time when there are 9.1 unemployed people in the Community, and the Commission has calculated that there are 30 million people living in poverty, of whom 10 million are 'very poor'.

The amount of agricultural goods that the Community needs to ensure its economic security is probably produced by that quarter of its farmers who have no need of income support. It does not make economic sense to subsidize agriculture to the point at which it can supply all the Community's needs, leave alone to the point at which it has to export. A country such as France should not expect the rest of the Community to pay so that it can arrest the decline of its agriculture (and reap balance of payments benefits), any more than the UK should expect the Community to pay for its failure to develop new industries. On the other hand, lower prices would enable the Community's agricultural exporters to recoup parts of the Community market, and to export more to the world market. It has been suggested within the German chancellor's office that Germany should be willing to import more agricultural goods from the Community if the CAP were reformed. The UK government should encourage and emulate this attitude. It could well meet with a favourable response from an exporting country such as the Netherlands, which is concerned to maintain its trade in the Community, and whose agriculture would be highly competitive at a lower price level.

The strands of agricultural policy need to be disentangled so as to facilitate decision-making. In agricultural policy, decisions are often made on political grounds, and a spurious economic rationale for them is invented subsequently. If the actual economic consequences conflict with the rationale, there is a tendency to tinker with them until they fit. MCAs are an example of a decision taken largely for political reasons which had far-reaching economic implications. These were neither foreseen nor properly understood when they happened, with the result that both the politics and the economics of MCAs became more complex than they need have been. Political considerations will probably continue to dominate agricultural policy for some time. The economic implications of a political decision should be taken into account, however, if only because they are likely to have political repercussions. Were this done more systematically, the CAP could come nearer to achieving the five objectives of the Treaty of Rome.

Tables

Table 1   Percentage share of agriculture in GNP and in total employment; ratio between output per worker in agriculture and in the total economy, selected years

	Percentage share of agriculture in GNP (at factor cost)			Percentage share of agriculture in total employment			Ratio between output per worker in agriculture and in total economy (%)	
	1968	1973[a]	1979	1968	1973	1979	1968	1979
Germany	4.4	3.1	2.1	9.9	7.5	6.2	44	34
France	7.5	7.1	4.8	15.7	11.1	8.9	48	54
Italy	10.7	8.6	7.5	22.9	18.3	14.9	47	50
Netherlands	6.9	5.7	4.1	7.9	6.8	6.0	87	68
Belgium	4.9	4.1	2.6	5.6	3.8	3.1	88	84
Luxembourg	4.6	3.9	2.8	9.9	8.1	6.4	46	44
UK	3.0	2.8	2.2*	3.5	2.9	2.6	86	85
Ireland	18.8	18.4	13.7	29.4	24.8	21.0	64	65
Denmark	7.5	6.6	4.8	12.8	9.5	8.3	59	58

[a]As of 1973, the series are based on figures exclusive of VAT (except Italy).
*Estimate
Source: The Agricultural Situation in the Community 1980 Report, p. 158.

Table 2   Annual percentage changes in value added, employment and productivity in agriculture, 1968-73 and 1973-78[a]

	Gross value added		Employment		Labour productivity	
	1968-73 at 1970 prices	1973-78 at 1975 prices	1968-73	1973-78	1968-73	1973-78
EC-9	1.3[b]	−1.5	−4.8[b]	−2.9	6.4[b]*	1.5
Germany	2.5	0.1	−4.9	−3.9	7.9	4.1
France	1.5	−1.4	−5.3	−3.6	7.1	2.3
Italy	−0.1	1.0	−4.7	−2.4	4.9	3.5
Netherlands	4.2	3.2	−2.6	−1.7	6.9	5.0
Belgium	1.6	−1.0	−6.4	−3.6	8.5	2.8
Luxembourg	0.2	−1.0	−5.3	−3.9	5.9	3.0
UK	–	−3.6[c]	−3.5	−2.0	–	−1.1[c]
Ireland	1.4	2.5	−3.4	−2.6	4.9	5.2
Denmark	−1.3	0.4	−4.8*	−1.2	−3.6*	1.7

[a] Figures for 1968 and 1978 are three-year averages
[b] Excluding UK.   [c] 1973-6.   *Estimate.
Source: The Agricultural Situation in the Community 1980 Report, pp. 168-9.

Table 3   Member states' share of gross value added (at factor cost) by
agriculture in the Community, 1978

Germany	19.4
France	28.0
Italy	26.2
Netherlands	7.3
Belgium	3.3
Luxembourg	0.1
United Kingdom	9.1
Ireland	2.7
Denmark	3.8

Source: Eurostat Review, 1970-1979.

Table 4   Member states' budget payments, receipts and net contributions, 1979

	Payments to budget*		Payments to member states†		Net contributions‡
	ECU	%	ECU	%	ECU
Germany	4407	30.7	2897	22.6	1510
France	2887	20.1	2846	22.1	41
Italy	1793	12.5	1830	14.2	−37
Netherlands	1344	9.3	1664	13.0	−320
Belgium	967	6.7	876	6.8	91
Luxembourg	19	0.1	15	0.1	4
United Kingdom	2514	17.5	1141	8.9	1373
Ireland	105	0.7	746	5.8	−641
Denmark	337	2.4	832	6.5	−495
EC-9	14,372	100.0	12,847	100.0	1526

*Net after financial compensations.
†Exporter benefits from MCAs.
‡Positive total net contributions reflects budgetary expenditures not paid to
member states, e.g. administration and overseas aid.

Source: Eurostat Review, 1970-1979.

Table 5 FEOGA and total budget expenditure, 1968–79

						Expenditure						
	1968	1969	1970	1971	1972	1973	1974	1975	1976	1977	1978	1979
Guarantee	815.6	1,876.6	2,287.4	1,219.4	3,948.8	3,174.2	3,277.9	4,821.4	5,365.0	6,166.8	8,672.8	10,434.5
Guidance	37.6	24.6	79.4	105.1	74.0	123.7	128.4	184.3	218.2	296.7	428.5	403.4
Total FEOGA	853.2	1,901.2	2,366.8	1,324.5	4,022.8	3,297.9	3,406.3	5,005.7	5,583.2	6,463.5	9,101.3	10,837.9
Total Budget	1,043.7	2,109.9	2,585.5	1,668.9	4,517.7	4,004.6	4,516.4	6,411.2	7,287.6	8,704.9	12,181.7	14,372.4
Guarantee as:												
% FEOGA	95.6	98.7	96.6	92.1	98.2	96.2	96.2	96.3	96.1	95.4	95.3	96.3
% Total	78.1	88.9	88.5	73.1	87.4	79.3	72.6	75.2	73.6	70.8	71.2	72.6
Guidance as:												
% FEOGA	4.4	1.3	3.4	7.9	1.8	3.8	3.8	3.7	3.9	4.6	4.7	3.7
% Total	3.6	1.2	3.1	6.3	1.6	3.1	2.8	2.9	3.0	3.4	3.5	2.8

Notes on sources:
1968:   From 1974 Audit Board Report.
1969–1977: From 1977 Audit Court Report.
1978:   From 1980 Draft Budget.
1979:   *Eurostat Review 1970–79.*

Adapted from *32nd Report of the Select Committee on the European Communities of the House of Lords*, Session 1979–80, p. 117.

Table 6 Breakdown of Guarantee Section appropriations by sector, financial year 1979 (m EUA)

Sector	Appropriations		Export refunds	Storage	Intervention		
	Sector total	As % of A+B+C			Price Subsidies	Other	Total Intervention
A– Cereals	1,563.7	15.0	1,184.7	88.9	290.1	–	379.0
Rice	42.9	0.4	41.7	–	1.2	–	1.2
Milk products	4,527.5	43.4	2,087.9	853.8	1,496.5	89.3	2,439.6
Oils and fats:	606.0	5.8	1.2	22.9	581.9	–	604.8
– olive oil	(388.2)	(3.7)	–	(22.6)	(365.6)	–	(388.2)
– oilseeds	(203.8)	(2.0)	(1.2)	(0.3)	(202.3)	–	(202.6)
– flax seed	(12.3)	(1.2)	–	–	(12.3)	–	(12.3)
Sugar	939.8	9.0	685.1	240.0	14.7	–	254.7
Beef and veal	748.2	7.2	270.2	417.2	0.5	60.3	478.0
Pigmeat	104.9	1.0	78.4	–	26.5	–	26.5
Eggs and poultrymeat	79.5	0.8	79.5	–	–	–	–

Fruit and vegetables	442.9	4.2	34.5	—	324.2	84.2	408.4
Wine	61.9	0.6	4.6	22.5	11.1	23.7	57.3
Tobacco	225.4	2.2	3.7	12.5	209.3	—	221.8
Other	389.3	3.7	260.7	—	137.1	8.5	145.6
Total A	9,732.1	—	4,732.2	1,657.8	3,076.2	266.0	4,999.9
%	100	—	48.6	17.0	31.6	2.7	51.4
B – Accession compensatory amounts in intra-Community trade	0.2	0	—	—	0.2	—	0.2
C – Monetary compensatory amounts							
– in intra-Community trade	458.8	4.4	—	—	458.8	—	458.8
– in extra-Community trade	249.6	2.4	249.6	—	—	—	—
Total A+B+C	10,440.7	100	4,981.8	1,657.8	3,535.2	266.0	5,458.9
%	100	—	47.7	15.9	33.9	2.5	52.3

Source: EC Commission, Directorate–General for Agriculture.

Table 7 Breakdown of expenditure by Guidance Section on common measures, 1975–79

		1978*	1979*	1975–79*	
		1000 EUA	1000 EUA	1000 u.a./EUA	%
I – *Common measures*					
Directive on the modernization of farms		28,019	54,277	107,980	18.5
Directive on the cessation of farming		251	353	765	0.1
Directive on socio-economic guidance		2,638	3,901	10,507	1.8
Directive on hill-farming		34,581	82,534	213,191	36.5
Aid to groups of hop producers		1,606	2,116	6,311	1.1
Conversion projects in the salt codfishing sector		—	—	7,038	1.2
Survey of potential production of fruit trees		3,336	588	4,266	0.7
Conversion to meat production		13,322	10,837	76,897	13.2
Survey on the structure of agricultural holdings		1,720	—	8,599	1.5
Premiums for the non-marketing of milk and the conversion to meat production		65,968	59,506	128,383	22.0
Conversion of vineyards		9,960	9,694	19,654	3.4
	Total	161,407	223,806	583,537	100.0

*1975–7: u.a.; 1978–9: EUA.

Source: EC Commission Directorate-General for Agriculture.

Table 8 National expenditure on agriculture, 1977 (million ECU)

Category	EC-9	Germany	France	Italy	Nether-lands*	Belgium	Lux	UK	Ireland*	Denmark
General measures	812.7	10.4	456.0	6.3	67.7	42.5	0.0	155.9	15.6	58.3
Production	2986.9	1152.9	660.8	412.3	151.3	99.1	23.4	384.8	51.4	50.9
Marketing and processing of agricultural products	475.5	67.3	135.4	75.6	44.5	7.4	3.9	93.7	27.1	20.6
Forestry and general development	86.6	17.5	47.4	5.0	n.a.	2.0	0.0	7.3	n.a.	7.4
Miscellaneous	821.7	0.0	805.6	6.6	—	0.0	0.0	9.2	—	0.3
Consumption	394.7	0.0	9.0	0.0	0.4	0.2	0.0	292.3	47.7	45.1
Tax relief	1757.8	426.7	195.5	0.0	52.5	0.0	0.1	1024.9	58.2	0.0
Total	7336.0	1674.8	2309.7	505.8	316.4	151.2	27.4	1968.1	200.0	182.6
State contribution towards financing of farmers' social insurance	6279.3	1299.1	3393.5	808.9	61.4	176.3	15.8	219.5	70.4	234.4
Total	13,615.3	2973.9	5703.2	1314.7	377.8	327.5	43.2	2187.6	270.4	417.0

Note: These figures in general include the national contribution towards measures adopted on the basis of Community provisions.

*1976

Source: The Agricultural Situation in the Community 1980 Report, pp. 244–5.

Table 9 Total number of farms and percentage in each size category in each member state, 1975

	EC-9	Germany	France	Italy	Netherlands	Belgium	Lux	UK	Ireland	Denmark
Farms (1000)	5084	905	1209	2053	144	106	6	272	260	130
%										
1-5[a]	41.9	34.5	20.5	68.2	24.9	29.9	19.2	14.3	17.3	11.9
5-10	17.4	19.8	15.3	17.5	21.3	22.2	12.2	12.5	18.2	19.3
10-20	17.6	23.4	22.7	8.4	30.6	27.0	18.4	15.9	31.1	28.3
20-50	16.8	19.5	29.9	4.1	20.9	17.8	40.9	26.8	26.0	32.7
>50	6.3	2.9	11.6	1.8	2.2	3.2	9.3	30.5	7.4	7.8
Total	100.0	100.0	100.0	100.0	100.0	100.0	100.0	100.0	100.0	100.0

[a] Hectares of utilized agricultural area.

Source: The Agricultural Situation in the Community 1980 Report, p.250.

Table 10   Share of agricultural trade in member states' total trade 1970 and 1979* (percentage)

	Imports		Exports	
	1970	1979	1970	1979
Germany	16.6	11.6	3.1	4.5
France	13.0	10.7	15.3	14.3
Italy	16.7	13.9	8.3	7.5
Netherlands	12.6	12.7	23.3	19.5
B-Lux	12.0	11.1	8.0	8.8
UK	22.8	13.7	6.4	6.8
Ireland	13.0	11.5	43.5	37.0
Denmark	9.3	9.9	35.5	31.9
EC-9	15.9	12.1	10.2	10.1

*Food, beverages and tobacco as percentage of total.
Source: Eurostat Review, 1970-1979.

Table 11   Member states' share in Community trade in agriculture, 1970 and 1979

	Share of Community agricultural imports		Share of Community agricultural exports	
	1970	1979	1970	1979
Germany	26.8	25.3	9.3	13.4
France	13.3	15.7	23.7	24.2
Italy	13.5	14.8	9.6	9.3
Netherlands	9.1	11.7	24.0	21.3
B-Lux	7.3	9.2	8.2	8.5
UK	26.6	19.2	10.8	10.6
Ireland	1.1	1.6	4.3	4.6
Denmark	2.2	2.5	10.2	8.0

Source: Eurostat Review, 1970-1979.

Table 12   Degree of self-supply in selected agricultural products, 1968/69 and 1977/78[a]

Produce	Year	EC-9	Germany	France	Italy	Netherlands	B-Lux	UK	Ireland	Denmark
Total cereals	1968/9	86	79	147	69	38	48	63	80	99
	1977/8	91	83	155	67	27	43	71	82	111
of which:										
Wheat	1968/9	94	86	154	95	54	59	45	68	103
	1977/8	105	98	185	78	62	72	65	56	139
Sugar	1968/9	82	89	117	93	101	148	34	94	124
	1977/8	117	123	183	91	153	208	37	121	190
Fresh vegetables	1968/9	98	53	95	112	182	112	78	101	92
	1977/8	93	33	92	117	117	113	73	102	72
Fresh fruit (excl. citrus)	1968/9	80	58	95	116	81	71	34	20	71
	1977/8	76	46	88	133	50	51	30	26	52
Wine	1968/9	97	56	92	110	2	11	0	0	0
	1977/8	99	60	97	127	0	7	0	0	0
Fresh milk (excl. cream)	1968	100	100	99	100	100	102	100	100	100
	1978	100	100	101	98	97	117	100	100	104

Skimmed milk powder[b]	1968	140	146	183	–	48	187	91	426	128
	1978	110	179	111	13	53	127	153	703	130
Butter[c]	1968	91	104	119	67	298	110	10	198	332
	1978	111	133	112	70[d]	481	110	38	283	273
Beef and veal	1968	90	87	109	63	109	89	61	590	252
	1978	97	98	106	61	129	93	74	578	315
Pigmeat	1968	100	95	87	88	171	130	58	162	495
	1978	100	88	84	76	224	169	63	144	357
Vegetable oils and fats[e]	1968	n.a.	7	20	43	–	1	n.a.	n.a.	n.a.
	1978	25	9	27	57	3	1	5	–	5

a 3-year average. b 1977 3-year average for EC-9 and Ireland. c Including butteroil. d Eurostat estimate.

e Average of 1977 and 1978, except Germany, UK, Denmark and EC-9 (average of 1976 and 1977). n.a. Not available.

Source: *The Agricultural Situation in the Community Report 1980*, pp. 204–5.

Table 13 Member states' intra-Community trade and total trade in agricultural products, 1973 and 1979

1973

	Imports			Exports			Balance	
	Intra	Total	Intra as % of total	Intra	Total	Intra as % of total	Intra	Total
Germany	4,577	10,151	45	1,753	2,817	62	-2,824	-7,334
France	1,766	5,645	31	4,075	6,089	67	2,309	444
Italy	2,650	6,876	39	1,048	1,659	63	-1,602	-5217
Netherlands	1,523	3,880	39	3,996	5,137	78	2,473	1,257
B-Lux	1,856	2,936	63	1,652	1,996	83	-204	-940
UK	2,589	8,639	30	880	2,167	41	-1,709	-6,472
Ireland	190	408	47	654	795	82	464	387
Denmark	220	979	22	1,240	2,029	61	1,020	1,050
EC-9	15,371	39,514	39	15,298	22,689	67	—	-16,825

1979

	Imports			Exports			Balance	
	Intra	Total	Intra as % of total	Intra	Total	Intra as % of total	Intra	Total
Germany	9,034	18,696	48	4,707	7,019	67	−4,327	−11,677
France	5,066	11,608	44	7,663	11,595	66	2,597	−13
Italy	5,606	12,275	46	2,814	4,373	64	−2,792	−7,902
Netherlands	3,542	8,502	42	8,497	10,897	78	4,955	2,395
B-Lux	4,183	6,327	66	3,421	4,220	81	−762	−2,107
UK	5,082	13,519	38	2,788	5,222	53	−2,294	−8,297
Ireland	723	1,040	70	1,653	2,032	81	930	992
Denmark	654	2,074	32	2,623	4,099	64	1,969	2,025
EC-9	33,889	74,041	46	34,164	49,454	69	—	−24,584

Source: The Agricultural Situation in the Community 1980 Report, p. 209.

Table 14 World trade and Community trade in the principal agricultural products[a]

1	World production 1000 t	World trade[b] 1000 t	(3/2) × 100 Proportion of production traded	% of world trade		
				Imported by EC	Exported by EC	(6−5) Net EC share of world trade
	2	3	4	5	6	7
Total cereals (except rice)	1,204,374	149,663	12.4	16.1	4.6	−11.5
of which: Total wheat	441,474	67,081	15.2	7.0	7.1	0.1
Feed grain (except rice)	762,900	85,582	10.8	23.6	2.6	−21.0
of which: Maize	362,971	59,219	16.3	26.7	0.1	−26.5
Oilseeds (by weight produced)	194,434	26,374	13.6	45.4	0.2	−45.2
of which: Soya	80,232	21,041	26.2	45.6	0.0	−45.6
Wine	28,641	2,496	8.7	21.6	27.0	5.4

Sugar	105,170	24,667	23.5	8.3	10.0	1.7
Total whole milk	457,501	147	0.0	0.7	62.6	61.9
Butter	6,972	540	7.7	23.3	36.7	13.3
Cheese	10,484	580	5.5	15.5	36.0	20.5
Milk powder (skimmed and whole)	6,692	1,296	19.4	0.3	49.7	49.4
Total meat (except offal)	113,438[c]	4773[d]	3.5[c]	17.8[c]	7.6[c]	−10.2[c]
of which: Beef and veal	48,141[c]	2016[d]	4.2[d]	7.8[d]	5.5[d]	−2.3[d]
Pigmeat	49,168[c]	496[d]	1.0[d]	19.6[d]	9.5[d]	−10.1[d]
Poultrymeat	25,828	676	2.6	7.5	27.8	20.3
Hens' eggs	25,666	305	1.2	5.6	11.5	5.9

Notes on sources: FAO (World production and world trade). Eurostat (% of world trade).
[a]3-year average 1976–8.   [b]Exports (excluding intra-EC trade and excluding processed products).
[c]Including salted meat.   [d]Excluding salted meat for trade.

Source: The Agricultural Situation in the Community 1980 Report, p. 202.

Notes

Chapter 2

1 See Nina Heathcote, *Agricultural Politics in the European Community*, Australian National University, Department of Political Science, Occasional Paper No. 7.
2 For a more detailed analysis of these points, see John Marsh and Christopher Ritson, *Agricultural Policy and the Common Market* (London: Chatham House and PEP, March 1971), ch. 2.
3 See Theodor Heidhues, *World Food: Interdependence of Farm and Trade Policies* (London: Trade Policy Research Centre, 1977), pp. 34–6.
4 The case for an indirect approach is explained in Pierre Uri, rapporteur, *A Future for European Agriculture: A Report by a Panel of Experts* (Paris: Atlantic Institute, 1971), p. 10. In support, the report quotes Napoleon's pronouncement: 'One has to have a plan, if for no other reason than to be able to change it.'
5 In 1977, for example, there were 1,548 voting procedures, of which 1,427 produced favourable opinions, 119 led to no opinion and two opinions were unfavourable. Commission of the European Communities, *The Agricultural Policy of the European Community*, 2nd edn (Luxembourg: Office for Official Publications of the European Communities, 1979), p. 29.
6 The decision-making process is outlined in Commission of the European Communities, *The Common Agricultural Policy* (Brussels, 1977), pp. 13–15.
7 The objective method is described in detail, its advantages and disadvantages discussed, in *Nineteenth Report of the Select Committee on the European Communities of the House of Lords*, Session 1980/1, vol. 2 (London: HMSO, 1981), pp. 1–4; hereafter cited as *19th Report*. See also pp. 27–8 of the same document.

Chapter 3

1 Support-buying and payment of export restitutions are carried out

within each member state by government departments, or by national bodies which have traditionally been involved in market management. They may, in turn, use private companies for work such as storing grain that has been bought in, and they have wide discretion in the practical arrangement of the policy, such as applying quality control.

2 Preferential arrangements permit various imports to enter the Community at a guaranteed entry price well above the price implied by the variable import levy, and ACP sugar to enter free of levy. In 1980 the main items were: 95,000 tonnes of butter from New Zealand and Australia; 15,000 tonnes of cheese from New Zealand and Australia; 55,000 tonnes of Emmenthal cheese mainly from Switzerland and Austria; 400,000 tonnes of beef and veal from various third countries, including several ACP states; and 1,288,000 tonnes of sugar from ACP states.

3 Consideration is not given here to variations in costs that arise from divergences among the economies of member states, e.g. differing interest rates.

4 For a more detailed analysis of the Mansholt Plan and its repercussions, see Marsh and Ritson, *Agricultural Policy*, pp. 142–61.

5 'Prospects for the Common Agricultural Policy in the World Context' in M. Tracy and I. Hodac, eds., *Prospects for Agriculture in the European Community*, College of Europe, Bruges Week 1979 (Bruges: De Tempel, Tempelhof, 1979), p. 431.

6 The current ceiling for the guidance section is EUA 3,600m for 1980–4: that is, an average of EUA 720m a year.

Chapter 4

1 Commission of the European Communities, *Stocktaking of the Common Agricultural Policy*, Bulletin of the European Communities, Supplement 2/75 (Luxembourg, Office for Official Publications of the European Communities, 1975), p. 15.

2 For further explanation of the difficulty of calculating and comparing farm incomes, see John S. Marsh and Pamela J. Swanney, *Agriculture and the European Community* (London: Allen & Unwin, for the University Association for Contemporary European Studies, 1980), pp. 60–3.

3 Denaturing is treating food, for example by adding dye, to make it unacceptable for human consumption so that it can be sold at a lower price for animal fodder.

4 The Commission, referring to the vulnerability of energy supplies, drew the conclusion that Europe 'cannot afford to rely on others for its food supplies and has the duty to exploit the richness of its soil'. Later in the same document it noted: 'Agriculture consumes directly and indirectly large quantities of energy and it has an urgent need for technologies which would allow it to reduce that consumption.' Commission of the European Communities, *Reflections on the*

Notes

Common Agricultural Policy, COM(80)800 (Brussels, December 1980), pp. 5 and 25.
5 The effect of farm price rises on food prices is discussed in *19th Report*, pp. 13-14.
6 Commission of the European Communities, *Report on the Mandate of 30 May 1980*, COM(81)300/3 (Brussels, 22 June 1981), p. 12.
7 See *19th Report*, p. 7.

Chapter 5

1 The Community has used various units of account. The CAP has had its own unit of account. Another unit of account was used for the Community budget until 1977, when it was superseded by the European Unit of Account. In March 1979 the European Currency Unit replaced all other units of account.
2 Green rates are also called representative or reference rates. An idiosyncratic argument against the term 'green pound' was advanced by Mr W. Ross speaking in the first House of Commons debate on the green pound, which had been initiated by Ulster Unionist MPs: 'The term "green pound" is not one that endears itself to many representatives of Northern Ireland because green is the colour of Republicanism and in the eyes of Unionists is associated with all the false claims made by Republicans over the Northern Ireland territory.' 31 July 1975, quoted by Wyn Grant, 'The Politics of the Green Pound 1974-79', *Journal of Common Market Studies*, vol. 19, no. 4 (1981), p. 324.
3 In practice there may be some price differences. One reason for this is that MCAs are generally derived from the intervention price, so that when goods are traded at higher prices, the MCA is less than the exchange-rate differential. It is important to bear in mind that the choice is between keeping the green and the market rates at par or allowing them to diverge, and that MCAs are a consequence of this choice. In common usage, it is said that a country has 'positive MCAs' or 'negative MCAs', rather than that it has not made its green rate follow its market rate up or down. This is convenient and reflects the attention that has been directed to the levies and subsidies that result from MCAs. In some contexts, however, it is misleading to obscure the nature of the choice. Evidence to the House of Lords Select Committee indicates that Ministry of Agriculture officials cannot always avoid these pitfalls:
'It is not the fixing of our green pound. What has happened is that the market rate has moved and as a result of this the positive MCAs have opened up and therefore, because we are net importers, we pay a net amount into the Community budget.' *19th Report*, p. 32.
4 R. W. Irving and H. A. Fearn, *Green Money and the Common Agricultural Policy* (Ashford, Kent: Centre for European Agricultural Studies, Wye College, 1975), p. 17.

5 In practice, green rates may be altered at shorter intervals if currency developments or national policy require it.

6 The depreciation of the weaker currencies against the unit of account overemphasized their market depreciation, since the unit of account was valued only against the joint float currencies, which were strong. However, because the unit of account was an un-weighted average, the appreciation of the Deutsche Mark, which was the strongest currency, was underemphasized. See C. Mackel, 'Green Money and the Common Agricultural Policy', *National Westminster Bank Quarterly Review*, February 1978, p. 37.

7 Greece also decided not to join the EMS, though the drachma is included in the calculation of the ECU.

8 The domestic relative prices of agricultural goods with respect to non-agricultural goods depend on several variables: the green rate, the market exchange rate, the domestic non-agricultural rate of inflation, and changes in common agricultural prices.

9 Subsequently, the domestic prices of all traded goods tend to fall if the currency appreciates.

10 Since other prices will change as a result of revaluation, there will still be a different reallocation and redistribution.

11 The fact that the Irish pound was until 1979 in a currency union with sterling inhibited Irish policy. Ireland's MCAs were always lower than those of the UK, however, and much lower from 1976.

12 See Grant, 'The Politics of the Green Pound', pp. 322-5.

13 Whether the UK was a recipient of these transfers was a matter of controversy. From 1976 MCAs were paid or charged in the country whose currency gave rise to them, except those for exports to the UK and Italy. These MCAs were paid in cash in the exporting country and attributed to it in FEOGA Financial Reports. The Commission and some member states contended that they should be considered a benefit to the importing country, and the Commission presented two sets of budget figures showing the alternative attributions of these MCAs. On the basis of the figures that attributed to the UK the MCAs on UK imports, other member states argued that the UK was a large recipient of MCAs and so should devalue the green pound.

14 See *Cambridge Economic Policy Review*, April 1979, ch. 2.

15 'Price Pledge on Danish Bacon if EEC Levy is Dropped', *Financial Times*, 28 January 1981.

16 'Claims for Subsidies in EEC are Disputed', *The Times*, 26 January 1981.

17 The central rates of the EMS currencies were adjusted twice in 1979, not at all in 1980, and twice in 1981.

18 The Treaty of Rome prohibits customs duties between member states 'and all charges with equivalent effect'. The European Court of Justice several times ruled that MCAs did not contravene the Treaty.

19 Commission of the European Communities, *Stocktaking of the*

Common Agricultural Policy, Bulletin of the European Communities, Supplement 2/75 (Luxembourg, Office for Official Publications of the European Communities, 1975), p. 38.

20 Commission, *Reflections*, p. 23.

21 Commission of the European Communities, *The Agricultural Situation in the Community 1980 Report* (Luxembourg: Office for Official Publications of the European Communities, December 1980), pp. 84–6. The UK's Minister of Agriculture has drawn attention to the difficulty of comparing tax data: though UK farmers receive sizable tax rebates, they pay more tax than those in France and Italy, who appear to be largely or wholly exempt from tax. See *19th Report*, p. 85

22 'National Aid Undermines Common Farm Policy', *Financial Times*, 15 May 1981.

Chapter 6

1 Commission, *Stocktaking*, p. 13.

2 The UK Government's change in poultry health regulations, which came into effect on 1 September 1981, is an example of such a barrier being used against an export benefiting from national aids in another country, namely turkey production in France.

3 Commission, *Reflections*, p. 7. National tax systems in many cases reinforce the regressive distribution of income in agriculture by giving favourable treatment to all farmers regardless of their income.

4 The index of regional income (average = 100) for the regions with the highest and lowest incomes in 1964-5 and 1976-7 was as follows (Commission, *Agricultural Situation*, p. 228):

	1964-5	1976-7		1964-5	1976-7
West Nederland	307	285	Basilicata	39	33
Wallonie	221	191	Marche	39	51
Picardie	207	210	Calabria	41	42
Schleswig Holstein	205	240	Molise	43	27
Champagne-Ardennes	184	223	Abruzzi	56	43

5 *19th Report*, p. 121.

6 Commission, *Agricultural Situation*, p. 198.

7 Net contributions to FEOGA can be misleading because they are not adjusted for budget expenditure or receipts that result from production or consumption in one member state but arise in another. The most significant example is the 'Rotterdam effect': the Netherlands' net budget contribution includes levies and restitutions associated with imports to, and exports from, other member states that pass through the port of Rotterdam.

8 It might be thought possible to use current rates of import levies

or of export restitutions interchangeably to measure the gap
between Community and world prices, but in practice this is not so
for various technical reasons. The Ministry presents its results in
two forms, one based on levies and the other on restitutions! See
J. M. C. Rollo and K. S. Warwick, *The CAP and Resource Flows
among EEC Member States,* Government Economic Service Working Paper No. 27 (London: Ministry of Agriculture, Fisheries and
Food, November 1979).

9 See C. N. Morris, 'The Common Agricultural Policy', *Fiscal Studies,*
vol. 1, no. 2, March 1980.

10 See C. N. Morris, *The Common Agricultural Policy: Sources and
Methods,* IFS Working Paper No. 6 (London: Institute for Fiscal
Studies, March 1980).

11 In this calculation, receipts from the agricultural sector are netted
out of the sums for FEOGA and the budget. The resulting figure of
55.7 per cent is smaller than the proportion of the Community
budget generally quoted as agricultural expenditure.

12 For a straightforward theoretical analysis and quantitative esti-
mation of the effects of the variable levy, see Gary P. Sampson and
Richard H. Snape, 'Effects of the EEC's Variable Import Levies',
Journal of Political Economy, vol. 8, no. 5, 1980. Reprinted as
Institute for International Economic Studies, University of Stock-
holm, Reprint Series No. 157.

13 During a visit to Australia in August 1981, the US Agriculture
Secretary said that the US was 'willing to try almost anything' to
convince the Community to change its agricultural subsidies policy,
which was threatening the world trading system. *Financial Times,*
18 August 1981.

14 Seventeen proposals published between 1969 and 1976 are analysed
and compared in H. Priebe, 'Diskussion unterschiedlicher Lösungs-
ansätze', in H.v.d. Groeben and H. Möller, eds., *Möglichkeiten und
Grenzen einer Europäischen Union. Band 6 Die agrarwirtschaftliche
Integration Europas* (Baden-Baden: Nomos, 1979), pp. 149–66. An
earlier attempt to compare suggested changes is Rosemary Fennell,
The Common Agricultural Policy: A Synthesis of Opinion, CEAS
Report No. 1 (Ashford, Kent: Centre for European Agricultural
Studies, Wye College, 1973).

Chapter 7

1 For a detailed analysis of the evolution of the Community budget,
see Helen Wallace, *Budgetary Politics: The Finances of the European
Communities* (London: Allen & Unwin, for the University Association for Contemporary European Studies, 1980), ch. 2.

2 Cmnd 4715, July 1971, para. 96, quoted in 'The UK's Contribution
to the Community Budget', *Economic Progress Report,* no. 118,
February 1980.

Notes

3 See 'The UK Contribution to the Community Budget', *Economic Progress Report*, no. 123, July 1980, and Trevor Parfitt, 'The Budget and the CAP: A Community Crisis Averted', *The World Today*, vol. 36, no. 8, August 1980.
4 The harmonized VAT base consists of a range of goods and services broadly corresponding to expenditure on consumption. It does not tally with the actual VAT base in any member state. Note also that contributions to own resources are not related to actual VAT receipts, and are independent of the differing VAT rates of member states.
5 See 'Des impératifs budgétaires vont-ils désintégrer la politique agricole commune?', *L'Européen*, nos. 193-4, July–August 1980.
6 This section is based on a forthcoming article.

Chapter 8

1 The argument here seems to be based on the assumption that to maintain common prices necessitates converging on high prices: 'Can one imagine Ireland accepting high prices for beef if it had to bear the consequences, or France backing high prices for cereals or sugar, or the United Kingdom high prices for butter?' p. 16
2 Two additional factors were the appreciation of the dollar, in which many agricultural products are priced in world markets, and the contribution being made by the UK to the budget in the form of import levies arising from its large positive MCAs.
3 Of the 434 members only 188 were present.

For Product Safety Concerns and Information please contact our EU
representative GPSR@taylorandfrancis.com
Taylor & Francis Verlag GmbH, Kaufingerstraße 24, 80331 München, Germany

www.ingramcontent.com/pod-product-compliance
Lightning Source LLC
Chambersburg PA
CBHW050524280326
41932CB00014B/2445